CELEBRITY
LIMERICKS

From Muhammad Ali
to Warren Zevon

Neil Dickinson

 **FriesenPress**

Suite 300 - 990 Fort St
Victoria, BC, Canada, V8V 3K2
www.friesenpress.com

ISBN
978-1-4602-5221-5 (Paperback)
978-1-4602-5222-2 (eBook)

1. Humor, Form, Limericks & Verse

Distributed to the trade by The Ingram Book Company

TABLE OF CONTENTS

Dedicated to Robin Williams

In a brilliant comedic career
He filled millions of people with cheer
Now his soul has been freed
So we wish him Godspeed
As he enters his final frontier

He broke in as a fellow named Mork
Who was seen from L.A. to New York
On a seventies show
That he did long ago
With an actress named Pam in support

After that came unbridled success
From the talent with which he was blessed
Many laughs he provoked
As he bantered and joked
He was truly the master of jest

But in drama he also excelled
In the highest esteem he was held
For his acting techniques
Drawing glowing critiques
As his fee and his bank account swelled

Robin Williams was born with a flair
Which made him a rich millionaire
But with all of his fame
And artistic acclaim
He was riddled with angst and despair

So we say 'Rest in Peace' to a guy
Who was sweeter than strawberry pie
Now the curtain's come down
On this actor and clown
Who's the apple of many an eye

Muhammad Ali

A man called Muhammad Ali
Was a genius, most folks would agree
In the prize-fighting game
He earned riches and fame
With his fists that could sting like a bee

Cassius Clay was his name long ago
As it was when the world came to know
His great skill in the ring
Where he reigned as a king
And established a new status quo

As a kid 22 years of age
With his friends making minimum wage
Sonny Liston he beat
Like a bum in the street
And the world, overnight, was his stage

Cassius Clay had begun an emersion
Then he had a religious conversion
And a new Muslim name
But along with this came
Some degree of disdain and aspersion

He beat Liston again in a bout
That was shrouded in mystery and doubt
Sonny seemed to have dived
When no punch had arrived
At his jaw or his eye or his snout

Many title defenses ensued
Where Muhammad beat many a dude
Then the government said
'Fight the commies instead'
He refused, then he promptly got screwed

After three years of fighting in court
For the right to be back in his sport
He resumed his vocation
With great excitation
And burgeoning public support

He was champ once again pretty soon
Still a hero, much like Daniel Boone
In some classics he fought
Where with pain he was fraught
And his fans ate it up with a spoon

With his craftiness, quickness and stealth
He attained adulation and wealth
When he still had his youth
Now he's long in the tooth
And he struggles a lot with his health

We should honor Muhammad Ali
As a man who has earned his degree
He's a legend for sure
And his place is secure
As the greatest there ever will be

Woody Allen

He can write, also act and direct
And he's earned lots of cash and respect
He is witty and smart
Very good at his art
And his step-daughter gets him erect

Woody Allen began writing jokes
In the fifties while learning the ropes
In the comedy game
To be droll was his aim
For the nightclubbing ladies and blokes

His films are too many to mention
Laced with irony, humor and tension
Quirky slices of life
That can cut like a knife
Some are smacking of anal retention

Woody's personal life is neurotic
And much like his films, episodic
Six times he's been hitched
Many women he's ditched
Some believe that he's semi-psychotic

Woody Allen is now very old
But still he is box office gold
Since the day he was born
Many hats he has worn
We've enjoyed all the stories he's told

Andre the Giant

A wrestler named Andre the Giant
In the ring wasn't always compliant
With the rules that applied
He was famous worldwide
And a whitey, unlike Kobe Bryant

He was born in a village in France
Where he often was looked at askance
He was gentle and passive
Yet stunningly massive
And quickly grew out of his pants

He was acromegalic at birth
Which led to great tallness and girth
Growing up as a freak
Made him timid and meek
With a shortage of gladness and mirth

But Andre discovered his mission
When he went to a wrestling audition
And was signed to a deal
To exploit his appeal
And develop his name recognition

Vince McMahon was the ring impresario
Doing shows in the States and Ontario
Who made Andre a star
With a custom-made car
In the wacky pro wrestling scenario

For the thousands of matches he fought
A shitload of tickets were bought
Bringing fortune and fame
In his chosen domain
Where he won much more often than not

He could drink 50 beers in one night
He was 88 inches in height
And at 500 pounds
Andre's strength knew no bounds
As he filled his opponents with fright

In the movies he played a few parts
And impressed with his natural smarts
Princess Bride drew applause
And a lot of guffaws
His performance stole millions of hearts

Andre died on a wet winter day
In a Paris hotel where he lay
In his giant size bed
Where a maid found him dead
Then a forklift done took him away

Lance Armstrong

A bicycle racer named Lance
Competed in very tight pants
He pedalled, then piddled
Some thought he was riddled
With drugs when he cycled in France

But he cited the tests that he passed
To affirm all the wins he'd amassed
He was deemed to be clean
Quite unlike Charlie Sheen
But today as a cheater he's cast

Fellow riders came forward to squeal
That his muscles where harder than steel
Due to junk he injected
That went undetected
From methods to mask and conceal

Lance opted to throw in the towel
Which amounted to tacit avowal
That he cheated indeed
Even though when he peed
Nothing foreign emerged from his bowel

Lucille Ball

A lady we knew as Lucille
Was oozing with gusto and zeal
In an acting career
Spanning many a year
She was lousy with comic appeal

She was raised in the city of Butte
In a family not rolling in loot
Her father died young
From a thing in his lung
So he never became an old coot

In drama school Lucy enrolled
As a teen who was brazen and bold
They told her to scram
When she flunked an exam
But she later was box office gold

She went to New York and played parts
Showing off her theatrical smarts
As she honed her technique
Barely earning her keep
Much like hundreds of other young tarts

She put enough money away
To pack up and move to L.A.
Where wannabe stars
Work all night tending bars
And audition for movies all day

In B movies Lucy impressed
With the talent with which she was blessed
Then TV came along
And was soon going strong
With great sponsors like Borax and Zest

In the 40's she landed a hubby
A Latino who sang in a clubby
They dated and wed
And had sex in their bed
When she gave him a quivering chubby

The tandem of Ball and Arnaz
In the era of be-bop and jazz
Soon were rife with success
With a swanky address
And no shortage of glitz and pizzazz

For years I Love Lucy amused us
Lucy's antics amazed and enthused us
From her role as a nut
Viewers busted a gut
With much pleasure and joy she infused us

After Lucy and Desi divorced
She embarked on a similar course
In the sitcom domain
On familiar terrain
Where her standing was soon reinforced

Lucy lived to be 78
In her life she had much on her plate
She passed on in L.A.
When her ticker gave way
And she met with her ultimate fate

Brigitte Bardot

There's a lady we know as Brigitte
With good looks she was rife and replete
When she burst on the scene
As a ravishing teen
Who was also quite gifted and sweet

She was born in the nation of France
In the city of lights and romance
Where artists hang out
And the food causes gout
And absinthe sends you in to a trance

Brigitte studied dance for a while
Then learned she could please and beguile
With the beauty and grace
Of her body and face
And her pouting, libidinous smile

So a modeling gig she pursued
And she chubbified many a dude
When she strutted her stuff
Barely hiding her muff
But she never would pose in the nude

Then in movies Brigitte would appear
And it soon was abundantly clear
She had talent to go
With her radiant glow
And her penchant to charm and endear

She's made 46 movies to date
Although none have been overly great
She's been typecast a lot
For the roles that she's got
But she's always had food on her plate

Now she's championing animal rights
She abhors when a deer's in the sights
Of a guy with a gun
Shooting varmints for fun
Lots of heated debate she incites

Chuck Barris

A wacky old fellow named Chuck
Once provided us many a yuck
With a show he produced
Many laughs he induced
With contestants who'd patently suck

He was born in the city of Philly
Where the weather in winter is chilly
He wrote 'Palisades Park'
Once he worked for Dick Clark
Then he moved to L.A. and got silly

Chuck created The Dating Game show
Which transfigured TV's status quo
Then The Newlywed Game
Brought him lots of acclaim
And a virtual truck load of dough

But The Gong Show was Chuck's greatest hit
Where most any untalented twit
Could appear on TV
For a nominal fee
'Til the panel compelled them to split

After that he produced other stuff
But the public had seen quite enough
Of his zany creations
And strange machinations
Thus ended an era of fluff

Barris claimed that he worked as a spy
Causing 33 people to die
But the CIA said
He was nuts in the head
With a desperate compulsion to lie

Clyde Barrow

There once was a fellow named Clyde
Who took stealing and killing in stride
He was nasty and mean
Like a kick in the spleen
'Til the day he was ambushed and died

Clyde Barrow was born south of Dallas
In a house not exactly a palace
He was bad as a kid
Lots of robbing he did
He was loaded with hatred and malice

He met Bonnie at age 21
And he showed her his unit and gun
She was clearly aroused
At his manhood she browsed
Then they started their life on the run

In a spree that encompassed 2 years
Which involved many bullets and beers
Clyde and Bonnie had fun
Like Attila the Hun
Who impaled all his victims with spears

They had money to spend at their leisure
And memories they'd cherish and treasure
But one morning in May
Many cops made them pay
With their lives for their moments of pleasure

There once was a fellow named Barrow
Who feathered his nest like a sparrow
With his hot looking dame
Seeking fortune and fame
While rejecting the straight and the narrow

Drew Barrymore

A former child actor named Drew
Has heredity up the wazoo
She grew up on the screen
She was wild as a teen
Often looked at askance and askew

She was born in to wealth and excess
Shiny cars and a fancy address
She began her career
In her very first year
On her pathway to acting success

In 'E.T.' Drew played Gertie and scored
Great reviews and an Oscar Award
Which led to more parts
In the cinema arts
As her fame and celebrity soared

She has also produced and directed
And is now well ensconced and respected
On the Hollywood scene
She's divorced from Tom Green
Whom she slept with and often erected

John Belushi

There once was a fellow named John
To whom many were magically drawn
For his singular style
And his mischievous smile
Then one day he was suddenly gone

Chicago is where he was raised
And embarked on the trail that he blazed
On a road to success
That was fraught with distress
His behavior was often depraved

1971 was the year
John began his comedic career
Second City employed him
The public enjoyed him
For how he could charm and endear

Then in Animal House John broke through
Playing Bluto, who hoisted a few
In a low budget flick
With some wonderful shtick
In his Hollywood movie debut

But the thing he's remembered for most
Is still seen every week, coast to coast
Live on Saturday Night
He was such a delight
On a show with no permanent host

In eight movies John also appeared
Some were bad, convoluted, or weird
But some were a hoot
And made money to boot
Due to characters John engineered

But his personal life was a mess
He had problems he wouldn't address
Then one horrible day
He was taken away
Leaving millions of fans in distress

Jack Benny

There once was a man known as Benny
Who saved every nickel and penny
He was silly and funny
And earned lots of money
But claimed that he didn't have any

Early on Benny's act was vaudevillian
And he played many hall and pavilion
But he switched to TV
Much like Fibber McGee
As a clown he was one in a million

The 50's gave Benny his chance
To do his unique song and dance
On his own TV show
Where his ratings would grow
With his skits and his comical rants

He had learned how to play violin
That he nuzzled down under his chin
Though he wasn't so hot
We enjoyed it a lot
As we had one more reason to grin

Jack adopted a singular word
That he said when frustration occurred
He said 'Well!' and we laughed
Even though it was daft
In old reruns it still can be heard

He died back in '74
20 years before Eva Gabor
But his legend endures
With its charms and allures
Which can still make us roll on the floor

Irving Berlin

A fellow named Irving Berlin
Wrote the music for Holiday Inn
White Christmas was one
Of the songs that were sung
Years ago, and has never worn thin

Belarus is where Irving was born
A nation that didn't conform
To a commie regime
Which was nasty and mean
And engendered much anguish and scorn

He moved to New York at age five
When his parents believed they could thrive
In the land of the free
So they sailed the North Sea
And an ocean to safely arrive

But life in The States wasn't great
There was often no food on his plate
Irving's Dad soon expired
Eight kids he had sired
And didn't leave any estate

So Irving and all of his sibs
Except for the babies in cribs
Went to work every day
For a pittance of pay
To buy food that would stick to their ribs

On the streets he heard songs played in bars
From singing and drums and guitars
And he suddenly knew
What he wanted to do
Was perform and to shoot for the stars

He worked as a song singing waiter
But knew there was something much greater
He was destined to do
As his eagerness grew
And he wanted it sooner than later

In vaudeville Berlin paid his dues
Singing songs to divert and amuse
But he soon paid his bills
Through his song writing skills
After paying his requisite dues

World War I interrupted his road
To success when he left his abode
To join the campaign
On a foreign terrain
He was proud to have carried his load

After that there was fortune and fame
And lots of artistic acclaim
He returned in fine form
And took Broadway by storm
Penning many a stylish refrain

All the music he wrote long ago
Is still earning plenty of dough
For Irving's estate
Since he met with his fate
As it's aged like a vintage Bordeaux

Yogi Berra

At birth he was Lawrence P. Berra
Who was born in the jitterbug era
His friends call him Yogi
He's now an old fogy
Like Charo and Chita Rivera

He was born in a Midwestern State
Where Cardinals step up to the plate
To swing at a ball
Every Summer and Fall
For exorbitant wages they make

In minor league ball Yogi starred
And was held in the highest regard
He signed with the Yanks
And moved up through the ranks
He was known as a bit of a card

In the majors he played 19 years
Impressing his coaches and peers
With his arm and his bat
In his pinstripes and hat
It was better than working at Sears

13 championship rings Yogi won
Before his career was all done
As a coach and a player
Who could have been Mayor
If ever he'd opted to run

Yogi's known for the wonderful quips
That often emerge from his lips
He gets quoted a lot
And more often than not
He prevails in a battle of wits

Chuck Berry

A musical legend named Chuck
On the stage often walks like a duck
Now he's wrinkled and gray
But he won't go away
In his time many chords he has struck

He was born in St. Louis, Missouri
Where he once faced a trial by jury
In a time of depression
And racial repression
He had to grow up in a hurry

Chuck enjoyed singing songs as a child
When his manner was civil and mild
But then as a teen
Not unlike Charlie Sheen
He was angry and easily riled

After serving three years for a crime
Rubbing elbows with losers and slime
He resolved to make good
And behave like he should
So he'd never do any more time

Chuck got wed to his future ex-wife
And built a respectable life
He bought his own house
With his newlywed spouse
But they later had marital strife

When the fifties arrived, so did Chuck
Who saw ways he could make a good buck
Rock and Roll was the rage
In this new day and age
So he opted to try out his luck

He played all the black clubs in his town
Often acting a bit like a clown
But his talent and style
And gregarious smile
Got him plenty of local renown

But later things suddenly changed
He recorded and wrote and arranged
A life-changing tune
Which made Chuck a tycoon
After he and his wife got estranged

Maybellene was that seminal song
And Chuck was a star before long
Making records galore
He was hard to ignore
And was known from New York to Hong Kong

Chuck's approaching his 90th year
So he's spending more time on his rear
In his stylish abode
When he's not on the road
Spreading music, nostalgia and cheer

Pete Best

Peter Best had a job as a drummer
But one day life would deal him a bummer
He was axed from his band
Which is not what he planned
And replaced by a young up and comer

Ringo Starr took his job on that day
And The Beatles were soon making hay
They invaded the States
And had steak on their plates
While Pete Best worked for minimum pay

It is said Pete believed it was John
Who decided he ought to be gone
And that Lennon conspired
For Pete to be fired
For being aloof and withdrawn

He felt sad and left out in the cold
When The Beatles turned vinyl to gold
They were treated like kings
And could buy diamond rings
From the singles and albums they sold

The 90's brought Pete consolation
When a Beatle-produced compilation
Made him very well off
He stepped up to the trough
For the cash and some late vindication

Humphrey Bogart

To his friends and his fans he was 'Bogie'
A star from L.A. to Nairobi
And all points in between
On the silvery screen
But he never became an old fogy

He was born in New York Christmas Day
Looked around and decided to stay
And become a great star
Just like Hedy Lamarr
In the roles he was destined to play

In the twenties he went to auditions
For various Broadway renditions
Gaining glowing reviews
He was paying his dues
In pursuit of much higher ambitions

He went west to L.A. for a chance
To make movies of crime and romance
And again he impressed
As he feathered his nest
Putting serious dough in his pants

In The Petrified Forest he starred
As a man who had little regard
Or goodwill toward men
He'd spent time in the pen
Where he'd go for a smoke in the yard

Maltese Falcon is where he portrayed
A hard boiled detective named Spade
Where a black statuette
Caused a fat man to sweat
And a few other guys to be slayed

Casablanca was likely the best
Of his movies, where Bogie impressed
In a brilliant portrayal
Of love and betrayal
In times of discord and unrest

To Lauren Bacall he was married
Two kids in her tummy she carried
And in spite of some strife
She's enjoyed a good life
Even after he had to be buried

In Key Largo they both had a part
In a movie both stylish and smart
Where a thug and his crew
Sat with nothing to do
With his girlfriend, a booze swilling tart

Many roles Humphrey Bogart fulfilled
And many libations he swilled
While he lived in our midst
In the work that he didst
Many villains and brain cells he killed

Bogie died in his 58th year
And the show business world shed a tear
For this man with a gift
Who could thrill and uplift
With his penchant to charm and endear

Napoleon Bonaparte

There once was a guy called Napoleon
Who was French, as opposed to Mongolian
Josephine was his wife
They had plenty of strife
Neither one ever heard of linoleum

He fought many a war with his neighbours
With cannons and muskets and sabres
And he won almost all
He was not very tall
He enjoyed all the fruits of his labours

As a soldier Napoleon shone
And he sacrificed many a pawn
On the chessboard of war
He's a legend of lore
Like the vicious and great Kublai Khan

But the War of the Sixth Coalition
Found him lacking enough ammunition
When his generals revolted
Napoleon bolted
To Elba to plan his next mission

One year later he came back to France
As he knew he had one final chance
To return to command
As the boss of the land
With an army to train and advance

He would rule for just one hundred days
Then go out in a glorious blaze
Waterloo was the site
Of his ultimate fight
Where his flag of surrender was raised

Sonny Bono

There once was a fellow named Sonny
Who was talented, crafty and funny
Once he partnered with Cher
Who had long flowing hair
And they both made a sh*tload of money

He was born in the Wolverine State
Where the hunters have moose on their plate
He did much in his time
In his youth and his prime
Then at age 63 met his fate

Sonny Bono moved west to L.A.
Where the Angels and Rams used to play
Rock and roll came along
And it rang Sonny's gong
This new music just blew him away

So he landed a job with Phil Spector
In the burgeoning publishing sector
He met Cher and they dated
And quickly they mated
She proved to be quite the erector

They began to perform and record
Songs that Sonny had cleverly scored
Soon with Cher's beauty pipes
They were earning their stripes
As their egos and bank accounts soared

'I Got You Babe' is still getting play
On radio stations today
It's an anthem for lovers
When under the covers
A song that just won't go away

They got married and soon had a kid
From the copious humping they did
In the mansion they bought
With much joy they were fraught
As they shopped for a carriage and crib

Sonny's marriage to Cher crashed and burned
For a southern fried rock star she yearned
But the duo played on
When their union was gone
And the custody case was adjourned

Sonny later decided to run
For a Congressman's chair, which he won
So he moved to D.C.
In the land of the free
Then his daughter turned in to his son

Sonny Bono slammed in to a tree
When he went to Nevada to ski
And he died from his wounds
But we still have his tunes
Which continue to fill us with glee

David Bowie

He was born with the name David Jones
Back in England, the home of The Stones
Where it rains every day
And much soccer they play
In the land of warm Guinness and scones

In the sixties young David began
A splendid career that has spanned
Many decades of song
And he's still going strong
Like Don Fagen, who formed Steely Dan

He's appeared in some movies as well
Some were stupid, but others were swell
He's arranged and produced
Both acoustic and juiced
And he's pretty, like Barbara Mandrell

David's sexual orientation
Has been fodder for much speculation
There's been many a dude
Make his trousers protrude
From significant chubbification

Though his sexual partners have varied
Two hot women this fellow has married
And two kids he's conceived
On the course he has weaved
That each one of his spouses have carried

David's lasted for many a year
On the path that he opted to steer
With his style and his skill
Though he's over the hill
He continues to charm and endear

Marlon Brando

There once was a fellow named Brando
Who was famous, like Tony Orlando
He was thin in his youth
Then got long in the tooth
And his waistline began to expando

He was born in a midwestern State
Where they always have corn on their plate
And the 'Huskers play ball
Every Winter and Fall
As their fans get all bent out of shape

Marlon's mother adored him a lot
But was also a terrible sot
His old man was demeaning
And often was screaming
With anger and spite he was fraught

Marlon dropped out of school and dug ditches
With other untaught sons of bitches
Then the acting bug bit
So he opted to split
For New York seeking glory and riches

He took classes and landed some parts
On the stage, where he stole a few hearts
Then he moved to L.A.
Where the Rams used to play
And the beaches are rampant with tarts

Then for 51 years Marlon showed
He could easily carry his load
Making movies galore
Both at home and offshore
From his opulent area code

The Godfather ranks as the best
Of the movies that feathered his nest
Many tickets were sold
For the tale that was told
All the critics and fans were impressed

He played Don Corleone, who was vicious
And more than a little pernicious
But also paternal
And strangely fraternal
Whenever he deemed it judicious

Brando's personal life was notorious
He was often described as vainglorious
But his gift was so rare
That his fans didn't care
If his conduct was not meritorious

Jeff Bridges

Jeff Bridges was born in L.A.
Before Liberace was gay
Where movies get made
And where starlets get laid
In exchange for a role they can play

His father, a fellow named Lloyd
In the 50's was fully employed
As an actor of note
Shooting scenes in a boat
That was often remotely deployed

For a movie career Jeff was keen
So he moved to New York as a teen
To hone his technique
And to learn how to speak
On TV or the silvery screen

After that came subordinate parts
In the finicky cinema arts
He sought fortune and fame
And artistic acclaim
With his rugged good looks and his smarts

Pretty soon came unbridled success
Lots of cash and a fancy address
For the parts he portrayed
And the style he displayed
With amazing aplomb and finesse

In The Last Picture Show he was great
As a horny young guy with a mate
And a good looking chick
In a black and white flick
That made plenty of dough at the gate

In Starman he showed his diversity
As an entity facing adversity
With humor and grace
In a faraway place
Where his future was fraught with uncertainty

The Contender was maybe the best
Of his films, where he truly impressed
As a man who gets back
At a Washington hack
Who was trying to feather his nest

In his music he also excels
Like Bo Diddley, The Kinks and Shirelles
As he strums and he sings
Lots of pleasure he brings
With the various stories he tells

Foster Brooks

A comedy genius named Foster
Did not win an Emmy or Oscar
But his stand-up routine
Earned him plenty of green
When he flaunted his drunkenly posture

Kentucky is where he was born
Where bluegrass and grits are the norm
And a young Cassius Clay
First began making hay
And the Summers are humid and warm

Foster started his lengthy career
And the course he was destined to steer
Reading news on the air
With a natural flair
Coming off well informed and sincere

When a thing called TV was invented
Which radio people lamented
Foster moved to L.A.
And decided to stay
To get famous and rich and contented

But success didn't come right away
There were dues he was needing to pay
And he paid them for years
Like his hundreds of peers
In pursuit of artistic cachet

Perry Como saw Foster perform
His routine and was taken by storm
So he offered a pact
As his opening act
And a star was summarily born

Pretty soon there were offers galore
And crowds that were shouting for more
Foster's drunken persona
From Maine to Tacoma
Caused people to roll on the floor

Foster died in his 90th year
And the comedy world shed a tear
For a master of mirth
Who was put on this Earth
To pretend to be wasted on beer

Mel Brooks

A funny old bugger named Mel
Is a writer, like Buddy Sorrell
Plus he acts and directs
For comedic effects
And at times he produces as well

He was born in The Empire State
As the baby of Jimmy and Kate
They came from Ukraine
For the freedom they'd gain
And the food they could put on their plate

As a boy Mel was sickly and weak
And his future appeared to be bleak
So he sharpened his wits
Writing music and skits
To avoid getting punched in the beak

Buddy Rich once taught Mel how to beat
On the drums with his hands and his feet
Later Mel went to college
To heighten his knowledge
And cruise for young ladies in heat

After that Mel was sent off to fight
In the war when no end was in sight
So to Europe he went
Where he lived in a tent
And awoke at the dawn's early light

He returned to New York after that
Where he rented a studio flat
And began playing gigs
Where the people took swigs
And put tips in his jar or his hat

For Sid Caesar he worked writing jokes
To amuse many ladies and blokes
When TV was a craze
In its earliest days
And they advertised liquors and smokes

He created the series Get Smart
With Don Adams assuming the part
Of a spy who was thick
It was wonderful shtick
And its ratings were good from the start

Then Mel Brooks made the Hollywood scene
Making films for the silvery screen
Blazing Saddles was funny
And earned lots of money
For Mel, life was rich and serene

Young Frankenstein also would score
As a spoof that we all still adore
High Anxiety too
Was a real smasheroo
Leaving all of his fans wanting more

James Brown

There once was a fellow named James
Who sang with a group called The Flames
He regaled us with funk
Long before there was punk
And had sex with a bevy of dames

He was born down in South Carolina
And later did concerts in China
As a child he was poor
His old aunt was a whore
Who each night rented out her vagina

As a teen James spent time in the pen
With hundreds of other bad men
Then he tried to go straight
Like the hair on his pate
But he often got faced in his den

In the 60's he'd go it alone
With a singular style he would hone
He was dripping with soul
To be rich was his goal
And to give many women the bone

With his style and his gravelly voice
He became black America's choice
When the whites got on board
James could not be ignored
And he soon could afford a Rolls Royce

But too often James got in to dutch
From the dope and the drinking and such
In the joint he did time
In his youth and his prime
Like the felons of Starsky and Hutch

Through the years he had many a hit
And got in to a lot of bad shit
James got high quite a lot
With his women he fought
And was mimicked in many a skit

In two thousand and six, Christmas Day
The Father of Soul passed away
He blazed many a trail
When he wasn't in jail
And he earned every dime of his pay

George Burns

George Burns was a show business great
In his time he had much on his plate
Starting out on the stage
For a moderate wage
With his wife, a remarkable flake

Nathan Birnbaum is how he was known
Before he became fully grown
And lit up a cigar
As a show business star
Like John Wayne and Sylvester Stallone

At age seven he dropped out of school
And sat in the street on a stool
Shining shoes so his mum
Wouldn't live like a bum
Back when movies were played from a spool

In the era of vaudeville he starred
And was held in the highest regard
Earning fortune and fame
After changing his name
He was known as the ultimate card

He married a woman named Gracie
Who acted more silly than racy
With the grace of a swan
'Til the day she was gone
They were close, much like Hepburn and Tracy

In the movies he also appeared
And consistently charmed and endeared
He was great in Oh God!
With no staff and no rod
And a ball cap instead of a beard

Now it's been many years since the day
That this talented guy passed away
At one hundred years old
He was box office gold
And well worth every dime of his pay

David Byrne

A fellow we call David Byrne
Has long been a going concern
With a wondeful gift
To divert and uplift
As his fame and his fortune affirm

He was born in the town of Dumbarton
A place where the locals wear tartan
To show off their knees
In a land overseas
From which David would soon be departin'

In Maryland David was raised
And embarked on the trail that he blazed
Over many a year
In his music career
He has constantly charmed and amazed

He quit college to play in a band
But things didn't go as he planned
Then he moved out of state
With Chris Frantz and his mate
To develop his sound and his brand

What ensued was unbridled success
Sold out halls and a fancy address
For a fellow with flair
Like the late Fred Astaire
And no shortage of wit or finesse

Talking Heads is the name David chose
For a group that he soon would expose
To fortune and fame
And artistic acclaim
Through their studio work and their shows

Sid Caesar

There once was a fellow named Sid
Who cracked people up as a kid
With his ethnic patois
He drew many guffaw
Now he lays in a morgue on a skid

Sid was keen for a music career
But it soon was abundantly clear
That it wasn't his thing
In the era of swing
Which was music to many an ear

But in comedy Sid was an ace
As a guy who could keep a straight face
While his audience laughed
He was great at his craft
By combining good humor with grace

Now the ultimate curtain's come down
On a guy who lived life as a clown
Who arrived long ago
As a regular joe
And departed a man of renown

John Candy

The actor that played Uncle Buck
Gave us many a genuine yuck
With his humor and smile
And his singular style
He was proud to be born a canuck

Second City is where he was trained
Where the budget was easily drained
They made wonderful skits
And the pay was the pits
But some pathways to fame were attained

He was brilliant as Johnny LaRue
As a blowhard who hadn't a clue
Many roles he created
And none seem out-dated
When reruns are shown on the tube

Then the movies became his pursuit
And they offered him plenty of loot
For his big screen appeal
Many scene he would steal
At his craft he was smart and astute

It was Splash where he gained notoriety
As a guy who was short on sobriety
In the film Summer Rental
His job drove him mental
And needing a break from anxiety

In Planes, Trains and Automobiles
He played Del, a companion of Neal's
In Stripes he was Dewey
The picture was screwy
And led him to more movie deals

His last movie, Canadian Bacon
Completed the journey he'd taken
Now full circle has come
For the late Harry Crumb
But his legacy won't be forsaken

Al Capone

There once was a man named Capone
Who became very rich and well known
For his murderous ways
And his tantrum displays
Where his nasty demeanor was shown

He loved baseball, the opera and whiskey
And business affairs that were risky
Also hot dogs and beer
He could make disappear
When he cheered for the Cubs at Comiskey

In Brooklyn, New York Al was born
Full of hatred and malice and scorn
He was rotten and cruel
He got kicked out of school
Then his parents were sad and forlorn

Al saw profits in hookers and booze
So after he paid all his dues
To Chicago he'd go
Where much liquor would flow
And he soon was as rich as Tom Cruise

Al had kind of a split personality
And occasional bursts of morality
He'd give money away
Early on in the day
Then by noon he'd arrange a fatality

He got jailed for evasion of tax
And he ended up serving the max
By the time he got out
He'd lost all of his clout
And he gave his accountants the axe

Now it's many long years since he died
With his family and friends at his side
He lived life as he chose
Then he turned up his toes
It's amazing he never got fried

Rubin 'Hurricane' Carter

There once was a man known as Carter
Who got in to some very hot water
When some people were killed
He was handcuffed and grilled
And his prints were inscribed on a blotter

It was June, in the year '66
In a district where hookers turn tricks
When four people got shot
And two suspects were sought
By authorities acting on tips

Rubin Carter was tried and convicted
But eye witness accounts were conflicted
And the local D.A.
Led the jury astray
With the way many facts were depicted

A group of Canadians fought
A verdict that clearly was fraught
With significant doubt
They were fearless and stout
And the media liked them a lot

Through his 20 long years in the slammer
The Canadians raised such a clamor
For judicial review
That they tried him anew
In a far more legitimate manner

Rubin Carter was finally freed
When a judge in New Jersey agreed
That this muscular dude
Had been royally screwed
As he never committed the deed

Rubin Carter passed on in his sleep
In his ultimate fight he got beat
Now his soul has been freed
So we're wishing Godspeed
To a man who was sold up the creek

Johnny Cash

There once was a fellow named Cash
Who was short on flamboyance and flash
But long on compassion
Great music he'd fashion
He also once grew a moustache

He was born in an Arkansas town
Where chickens are often put down
And de-feathered and sold
To be served hot or cold
Or fried up to a deep golden brown

John began writing tunes as a teen
For a singing career he was keen
Then at age 25
His big break would arrive
When Sun Records arrived on the scene

Johnny Cash soon was bigger than life
With June Carter, his song writing wife
They had loads of success
And a fancy address
But they also had serious strife

Johnny conquered much pain and affliction
And many long years of addiction
He sang for the losers
The druggies and boozers
With empathy, zeal and conviction

Harry Chapin

There once was a fellow named Harry
Who was known for the tunes he could carry
And the words he composed
On the path that he chose
He was gentle and often contrary

Harry Chapin was born long ago
In the city where wannabes go
For Broadway auditions
With primal ambitions
Of finding producers to blow

In his youth Harry sang in the choir
In pursuit of his burning desire
To perform on his own
When his body had grown
And be someone his kids could admire

After high school he went to Cornell
But for only a very short spell
Then without a degree
He sang songs for a fee
'Til the day of his final farewell

With his brothers he played and recorded
Many rosy reviews were accorded
But Harry was keen
To be making the scene
On his own and be solely rewarded

With 'Taxi' he scored his first hit
A tale of a couple who split
But their paths later crossed
And they found what was lost
In a song we still hear quite a bit

After that came a stellar career
Where he sang of the sadness and cheer
Of the human condition
He reached his fruition
Then sadly no longer was here

Harry sowed so that others could reap
Such as people with nowhere to sleep
He donated so much
To good causes and such
That he lived his own life on the cheap

Harry Chapin expired too soon
And he never became a tycoon
But his music remains
Very etched in our brains
As it will be for many a moon

Graham Chapman

Graham Chapman made plenty of hay
As a guy who turned out to be gay
He found fortune and fame
In the comedy game
Then too soon he was taken away

He was born in the City of Leicester
When his Mom did her final trimester
And gave birth to a boy
Full of wonder and joy
Who grew up as a consummate jester

Early on he was drawn to The Goons
For their ribald and witty lampoons
Of life in Great Britain
So cleverly written
By splendidly wacky buffoons

After college he joined BBC
Writing skits for a nominal fee
When John Cleese joined the team
They developed a scheme
For a show of their own on TV

Monty Python came in to fruition
And many showed up to audition
For a part in a show
That was destined to grow
Like a babe in a fetal position

Graham Chapman won millions of hearts
With his writing and comical smarts
He mastered his craft
Being wonderfully daft
In his strikingly ludicrous parts

The Pythons made movies as well
And performed on the stage for a spell
Graham always had fun
With the humor they spun
In the era of Coco Chanel

But he also had demons to fight
He was prone to get drunk every night
On whiskey and beers
And it troubled his peers
But he later converted to Sprite

Graham died in his 49th year
But continues to charm and endear
On the reruns we see
Which infuse us with glee
And induce us to smile ear to ear

Dick Cheney

A wily old bugger named Dick
Had a boss who was stunningly thick
In his time as V.P.
Most observers agree
He was truly an infamous prick

He was born in the Cornhusker State
He managed a war in Kuwait
For Bush number one
Then he worked for his son
Who had many a negative trait

In college Dick earned a degree
And later moved east to D.C.
With his daughter and spouse
And he served in The House
Passing laws in the land of the free

Five straight times he obtained a deferment
To avoid getting shot or internment
In a place known as Nam
Not too far from Siam
He was rife with self-serving discernment

But he later sent others to fight
In a war that was clearly not right
And was based on a lie
Many thousands would die
Or come home with no hearing or sight

Cheney knew how to feather his nest
With political smarts he was blessed
Soon he wielded much sway
Like his friend, Tom DeLay
As his climb up the ladder progressed

Then came eight rather horrible years
When Dick Cheney and Bush and their peers
Stole at least one election
With lies and deception
And acted like true racketeers

Cher

A lovely old lady named Cher
Is known for her glamor and flair
In the show biz domain
Using only one name
And a massive collection of hair

She was born in a southwestern State
In the era of video tape
When the radio played
Vinyl discs that were made
And Rock Hudson was thought to be straight

Cher performed at a very young age
She yearned to be seen on the stage
Or in movies galore
Where she later would score
As a co-star with Nicolas Cage

She quit high school and moved to L.A.
To put all her skills on display
She was hired to dance
She looked good in tight pants
In a setting of moral decay

Cher hooked up with a fellow named Bono
When pre-marital sex was a no-no
She moved in as his maid
But was soon getting laid
Back when music was played on a phono

With Sonny she formed a duet
And recorded on tape and cassette
And plastic LPs
They were busy as bees
With a marriage they'd later regret

Cher and Sonny got famous and rich
But then their careers hit a glitch
When they went separate ways
With a daughter to raise
Who was seeking her sexual niche

Cher went solo and blew us away
Selling out from New York to L.A.
And points in between
She was living the dream
Of success in the U.S. of A.

In the movies she's also excelled
In the highest esteem she is held
Making many a scene
For the silvery screen
As her ego and bank account swelled

Julia Child

A lady named Julia Child
Cooked up dishes both spicy and mild
With much passion and glee
Every week on TV
Where she constantly charmed and beguiled

Pasadena is where she was born
Where the the summers are humid and warm
Her parents had loot
And upstanding repute
In her side they were never a thorn

In high school she stood 6 foot two
So competitive sports she could do
She played tennis and hoops
Long before she made soups
Baked lasagna and venison stew

After college she worked writing ads
Which publicized goods by the scads
Then she served in the war
Off the Indian shore
In support of some brave fighting lads

Julia married Paul Child after that
And in Paris they rented a flat
Cordon Bleu showed her how
To make wonderful chow
In a stylish French apron and hat

For a decade in Europe she wrote
Soon becoming a person of note
In the field of cuisine
On the restaurant scene
Where she often was asked for a quote

She continued to write in the States
About food people eat from their plates
Then she went on TV
So that millions could see
How to cook for their families and mates

With her singular manner and style
She caused millions of viewers to smile
As they learned to prepare
What she made on the air
When TVs had a manual dial

Julia died in her 93rd year
After spreading unlimited cheer
And much knowledge as well
Helping others excel
In the wonderful time she was here

Julie Christie

A talented actress named Julie
From the nation of Anthony Newly
Has earned fortune and fame
And artistic acclaim
And has chubbified many a tooly

In India Julie was born
Where saris and turbans are worn
Her Dad peddled tea
For a nominal fee
Long before there was internet porn

She was raised in the land of Great Britain
Where many are openly smitten
With Princes and Queens
And with toast served with beans
And where drinking warm beer is befittin'

In drama and speech she was trained
Where significant knowledge was gained
In the theatre arts
Where her talent and smarts
Brought her cash and artistic acclaim

Billy Liar was Julie's first break
Among all of the movies she'd make
Then in Darling she strayed
In the part she portrayed
As a truly libidinous flake

In Dr. Zhivago as Lara
She was hotter than Guadalajara
Though the movie was long
Julie Christie was strong
And established herself as a star-a

Shampoo was a splendid diversion
Where a hairdresser's member would burgeon
And get visibly fat
At the drop of a hat
Though he never had sex with a sturgeon

In Miss Mary she played a young nanny
Who aroused a young man with her fanny
And her face and her rack
So his Mom blew her stack
Her performance was truly uncanny

Don't Look Now was both stylish and weird
Back in '73 it premiered
Julie's daughter is dead
But she then reared her head
Donald Sutherland also appeared

Julie Christie had much on her plate
While amassing a healthy estate
With her beauty and skill
Now she's over the hill
But can still make a fella inflate

Eric Clapton

He arrived in the nation of Britain
Where many great songs have been written
And Shakespearean plays
Once drew critical praise
And where drinking warm beer is befittin'

Eric started to play the guitar
Long before he could drink in a bar
Or fight in a war
Or have sex with a whore
Or go driving around in a car

With The Yardbirds, and later with Cream
He followed his musical dream
On the path that he's steered
He has charmed and endeared
And is held in the highest esteem

With both fame and success he is rife
But he's also had anguish and strife
'Tears in Heaven' he wrote
As a posthumous note
To his son, at the end of his life

In August of '76
Eric got himself in to a fix
With a nasty oration
That sparked indignation
When prejudice spewed from his lips

But through all of the highs and the lows
And the staging of thousands of shows
In a 50-year span
He's no flash in the pan
And a star from his head to his toes

Kurt Cobain

There once was a man called Cobain
Who possessed a remarkable brain
He expired this date
In The Evergreen State
In a moment of anguish and pain

He fronted a band called Nirvana
And performed as the group's top banana
Earning fortune and fame
And artistic acclaim
They were big, like the sky of Montana

Kurt was born near the town of Seattle
Where the Seahawks and Mariners battle
And where earthquakes occur
Which most locals endure
While some others pack up and skedaddle

As a youth he was sadder than most
Often moving from pillar to post
He was sickly as well
In a childhood from hell
On the blustery Washington coast

Then music came in to his life
Relieving a lot of his strife
With his skill on guitar
He got known near and far
With both money and fame he was rife

When alternative rock reared its head
Kurt was making a shitload of bread
As the master of grunge
Who'd be taking the plunge
When he found a nice lady to wed

Courtney Love was the gal that he chose
She was cool from her head to her toes
And musically gifted
His spirits she lifted
But often sucked dope up her nose

While Cobain also battled addiction
From the street and obtained by prescription
His commercial success
Caused him angst and distress
And a feeling of mental confliction

As a talent Cobain had it all
He could truly astound and enthrall
On the trail that he blazed
All the world was amazed
From L.A. to New York to Nepal

Howard Cosell

A fellow named Howard Cosell
Had an ego that often would swell
He was truly unique
In his broadcast technique
And was great entertainment as well

He was raised long ago in New York
By a family who never ate pork
As it wasn't allowed
Howard cried very loud
When a Moyle took a knife to his dork

In college he earned a degree
In the law, then charged people a fee
For legal advice
That was clear and precise
Long before he appeared on TV

In the 40's he fought in the war
'Til the krauts couldn't take any more
When the constant attacks
Made it hard to relax
And the allies were storming the shore

Howard knew many people in sports
From helping them out in the courts
And it led to acclaim
In the broadcasting game
Where he started with on-air reports

With his knowledge and stunning verbosity
Howard went from a strange curiosity
To a star in his trade
Who was handsomely paid
For his gift of astute bellicosity

Ann Coulter

A middle aged lady named Ann
Is clearly no flash in the pan
But almost as clearly
She loves herself dearly
Much more than she loves any man

Ann's opinions are far to the right
And her bark is as mean as her bite
She will speak for a fee
She's as tall as a tree
And she's lousy with venom and spite

She was born in the Empire State
Where the Rangers and Islanders skate
She was trained in the law
When it filled her with awe
Then decided it wasn't so great

Federal politics jazzed her a lot
So she opted to give it a shot
She planned a campaign
And it failed to sustain
But she didn't get sad and distraught

Coulter later discovered her niche
And a way to get totally rich
In the publishing game
She found wealth and acclaim
Just by being a backstabbing bitch

She also gives speeches for loot
For people who think she's astute
With her self-serving drivel
That's mostly uncivil
And semi-psychotic to boot

Truth be known, all her shtick is an act
Based on show business rather than fact
It's her job to annoy
Not fill people with joy
Or display any semblance of tact

Bill Clinton

He's remembered by some as sublime
And by some as a cad and a slime
But we all can concur
That one thing is for sure
He's the horniest prez of all time

He was born in a town known as Hope
And admits once he puffed on some dope
When he studied at Yale
But he didn't inhale
Then he washed out his mouth with some Scope

Bill is wed to a lady named Hillary
Once a second banana ancillary
But now she's a shaker
A policy maker
And scary, like loaded artillery

Clinton won many major elections
With his wit and his charm and connections
He wrote many laws
But was known for some flaws
Like a bent for untimely erections

In the White House eight years he would serve
With demonstrable spirit and verve
But a stain on a dress
Got him in to a mess
Many called him a jerk and a perv

Yet his legacy seems to be strong
As a man who addressed what was wrong
Both at home and abroad
He's a guy we'd applaud
But he should've packed ice on his dong

Hillary Clinton

There is an old woman named Hillary
Whose role has been mainly ancillary
Serving two different chiefs
As they shook in their briefs
She was scary, like loaded artillery

She is wed to a horny old dude
And a lot of young babes he has wooed
Also middle aged skanks
Much to Hillary's angst
It's amazing he's never been sued

Back in Arkansas, Bill and his wife
Caused a lot of vexation and strife
With their shady affairs
And their trading in shares
With corruption and graft they were rife

As First Lady she served for 8 years
Through some difficult blood, sweat and tears
To the Senate she went
Like a hound with a scent
Where she frightened her minions and peers

Later Hillary sought nomination
For the chance to be running the nation
As Commander-in-Chief
In her honest belief
She could win and achieve validation

She got beat, to her great disappointment
But received a high level appointment
To reduce her disdain
And diminish her pain
Like Ben Gay or some other such ointment

Now she patiently waits for a shot
At the office she covets a lot
Which she likely will win
If she's able to spin
All the negative baggage she's got

George Clooney

George Clooney arrived one fine day
In the State where a young Cassius Clay
Made his boxing debut
Beating kids black and blue
As an amateur earning no pay

Clooney comes from a show business clan
And he knew as a very young man
What career would be best
For the skills he possessed
Which he showed later on in Roseanne

In Centennial George got his start
Where he played an irrelevant part
As his resumé grew
More attention he drew
As he quickly developed his art

Booker Brooks was his first major role
On Roseanne, which was clever and droll
Where a fat man and wife
Dealt with friction and strife
At The Lobo, a watering hole

Then a role on ER came his way
And a sizable increase in pay
Soon his work would be seen
On the silvery screen
Where he's made some significant hay

After Batman and Robin, he played
Archie Gates, who conducted a raid
To make off with some gold
In a plan that was bold
Where a bunch of Iraqis got slayed

Oh, Brother, Where Art Thou? was splendid
In a startling manner it ended
When a lake was induced
Joel Coen produced
Once again Clooney's work was commended

George has made 60 movies thus far
As a writer, director and star
Now at age 53
In the land of the free
He's considered a Hollywood czar

Nat King Cole

There once was a fellow named Cole
Who played many a watering hole
When he wasn't well known
For his wonderful tone
In the era before rock and roll

Alabama is where he was born
Back when blacks were regarded with scorn
And The Klan went around
Burning homes to the ground
Making people all sad and forlorn

To Chicago he moved with his kin
Where the color of somebody's skin
Wasn't such a big deal
When they went for a meal
Or to bars for a tonic and gin

He showed musical flair as a lad
And was urged by his Mom and his Dad
To follow his heart
And develop his art
With the natural talent he had

With his brother he started a band
That was soon very much in demand
In the clubs and the bars
They were treated like stars
And some studio sessions were planned

In L.A. someone called him 'The King'
For the grandeur with which he would sing
With the velvety sound
He was rightfully crowned
And he soon had the world on a string

At this time no one owned a TV
As it hadn't as yet come to be
So radio shows
Is where people exposed
Many talents that no one could see

Nat King Cole soon was top of the heap
And no longer lived life on the cheap
Selling out every show
Made his bank balance grow
And his pockets increasingly deep

A long time ago Cole expired
But still he is widely admired
For his great vocal style
And his radiant smile
And the genuine joy he inspired

Sean Connery

He's officially known as Sir Sean
But much better as Agent James Bond
He was born on this day
And has not gone away
On the chessboard of life he's no pawn

In Scotland Sean Connery arrived
As a baby his father contrived
When he used no protection
To shield his erection
And some of his swimmers survived

Sean's first job was delivering food
To many a lady and dude
On his dairy truck route
In a silly white suit
Long before he was dashing and lewd

In the Navy young Sean did a hitch
But his health caused a serious glitch
So they told him to scoot
And they gave him the boot
Then he later discovered his niche

He landed a role in a play
With no lines and for very low pay
But his talent shone through
So his salary grew
When the spotlight was shining his way

It was then that he met Michael Caine
Who also found fortune and fame
With the films that he made
In the thespian trade
To much critical freaking acclaim

Sean then moved to the town of L.A.
Where he found many women to lay
As a handsome young stud
Like Paul Newman in Hud
He was constantly humping away

In the States he would struggle at first
Even though he was fully immersed
In honing his craft
In the town of George Raft
It appeared that his bubble had burst

But then came the role that defined him
When a Hollywood studio signed him
To film Dr. No
For a truckload of dough
So he put all his humping behind him

In From Russia With Love he reprised
The role of James Bond he'd devised
With his license to kill
There was many a thrill
And some hooters befittingly sized

Then Goldfinger hit the big screens
And included some wonderful scenes
Like a girl painted gold
It was great to behold
And caused bulges in millions of jeans

Later Sean said good-bye to James Bond
Of whom all of his fans were so fond
He made many more flicks
But we still get our fix
When the Late Show has Thunderball on

Jimmy Connors

A man that we call Jimmy Connors
Has won numerous titles and honors
In tennis he ruled
Many rivals he dueled
With most ending up being goners

He was born in to privilege and cash
And grew up to be stylish and brash
On the court he was great
Each opponent he'd hate
Such as Borg or the late Arthur Ashe

With Chris Evert he once was an item
Her hooters both served to delight him
But they suddenly split
Then she married a Brit
To her wedding she didn't invite him

Jimmy later wed Patti McGuire
Who filled him with lust and desire
Once for Playboy she posed
But that chapter got closed
When he told her it's time to retire

But enough about Jimmy's libido
And how he let Chrissie torpedo
The course they had mapped
Which abruptly was scrapped
When she looked really hot in a Speedo

Over one hundred matches Jim won
Often sweating all day in the sun
He was king of the hill
Never run-of-the-mill
And he always appeared to have fun

So in verse I pay tribute to Jim
Who was full of much gusto and vim
When he played on the courts
In his lily white shorts
Back when tennis was boring and prim

Stompin' Tom Connors

A singer/composer named Tom
Was conceived when his Dad and his Mom
Had carnal relations
With no obligations
Then rinsed themselves off in the john

Tom's parents would never get wed
Right away his old man up and fled
The scene of his crime
Then his mother did time
When a verdict of 'guilty' was read

To Prince Edward Island he went
To live with a lady and gent
Who adopted the boy
As their bundle of joy
In a pre-arranged blessed event

Tom left home at the age of fifteen
To travel the land he was keen
So he stuck out his thumb
And lived life as a bum
Eating meals from a vending machine

When in Timmins a bar offered Tom
Some drinks if he'd sing them a song
Since his gullet was dry
He was quick to comply
Soon the locals were singing along

That gig lasted more than a year
Starting out with a shot and a beer
By the time he left town
As a man of renown
He was music to many an ear

As his travels continued he won
Many friends with the ditties he sung
In the bars and hotels
With their sights and their smells
Many wonderful stories he spun

With no drummer for keeping the beat
Tom began to make use of his feet
He stomped as he sang
With his Maritime twang
And a style that was fresh and unique

He sang for the regular joes
About all of the highs and the lows
In our everyday lives
For the husbands and wives
Drinking lager and tapping their toes

He wrote hundreds of songs in his time
In a genre that's hard to define
He was country and folk
He was quick with a joke
And a master of rhythm and rhyme

50 albums were also conceived
By this man who was widely perceived
By his fans near and far
As a bright shining star
For the wonderful things he achieved

Alice Cooper

To the tunes of a young Alice Cooper
We smoked ourselves in to a stupor
As we sucked on some brew
When his music was new
Back when nobody owned a computer

He was born in the Wolverine State
Where the great Gordie Howe used to skate
And where Motown made hits
To compete with the Brits
And had many great acts on their plate

Heavy Metal was new back when Alice
Embraced its irreverence and malice
He hooked up with a band
Who'd been boring and bland
Went on stage and drank blood from a chalice

Soon his talent and face were well-known
And his story was in Rolling Stone
But the drugs and the drink
Put his world out of sync
And he found himself living alone

But the demons went out of his life
Along with the anguish and strife
Now he's sober and clean
Since the Reagan regime
And he's back with his former ex-wife

Lou Costello

There once was a fellow named Lou
Who never went dirty or blue
When he made people laugh
He was good at his craft
And had silliness up the wazoo

In New Jersey Costello was reared
Where mafia hit men are feared
And people get killed
When a contract's fulfilled
And Sinatra was loved and revered

Early on Lou aspired to be
A guy who could make people pee
In their pants from his antics
And gift for semantics
For more than a nominal fee

After high school he moved to L.A.
Found some work and decided to stay
Soon he carved out a niche
And became rather rich
From the comedy roles he could play

He teamed up with a comic named Bud
Who up until then was a dud
They created some skits
With their wiles and their wits
When John Wayne was a Hollywood stud

'Who's on First' was a great piece of jest
Which many believe is the best
That ever was done
In the annals of fun
Full of wonderful comic finesse

Lou Costello showed wonder and glee
When we saw him on film or TV
With his deviant mind
He was one of a kind
Such a jolly good fellow was he

He expired a long time ago
When life's curtain came down on his show
He was great in his time
With his partner in crime
And was always a consummate pro

Jim Croce

There once was a fellow named Jim
Who was full of much vigor and vim
Then was gone in a flash
When he died in a crash
Causing grief for his fans and his kin

He arrived in the city of Phillie
Nine months after his Dad used his willy
To impregnate his Mum
As he fondled her bum
On a day she was not on the pilly

In college he studied psychology
And started his music chronology
Performing in pubs
For young babes and their studs
Who were keen for each other's biology

Jim met Ingrid and soon they were wed
Before he earned shitloads of bread
They lived on a farm
For the quiet and charm
Three years later poor Jim would be dead

But in the short time he was here
In his brief but successful career
He stole millions of hearts
With his songs on the charts
And was music to many an ear

Almost 300 concerts he played
Where his talent and warmth were conveyed
And with five top-10 hits
People loved him to bits
And his welcome was never outstayed

Russell Crowe

A fellow we call Russell Crowe
Gets a positive revenue flow
And artistic acclaim
From the show business game
Where he's known as a consummate pro

In New Zealand this fellow was born
Where farmers raise sheep to be shorn
Or slaughtered for meat
Which is tasty to eat
When it's served with potatoes and corn

Russell also spent time in Australia
Where natives wear gaudy regalia
And a model named Elle
Causes manhoods to swell
With her rack and her nice genitalia

He dabbled in music at first
But then he developed a thirst
For performing in plays
Like a young Helen Hayes
Who was later shipped off in a hearse

Down under Russ did very well
And he started enjoying the smell
Of artistic success
So he changed his address
Then his bank account started to swell

He moved to the U.S. of A.
For the prominent roles he could play
On the Hollywood scene
Not unlike Charlie Sheen
Who's the champion of moral decay

He was great in L.A. Confidential
A film that is deemed quintessential
In the genre of 'noir'
He arrived as a star
As he strengthened his earning potential

In Mystery, Alaska he played
A man who is clearly dismayed
When he's cut from his team
And deprived of a dream
When his energy started to fade

Later on, in A Beautiful Mind
He played John, who was one of a kind
In terms of his brain
But went slowly insane
When he lost all his reason and rhyme

Billy Crystal

A funny old bugger named Billy
Is an actor, like Jennifer Tilly
Since the day he was born
Many hats he has worn
But he mostly enjoys being silly

New York City is where he arrived
As a baby his parents contrived
On a hot summer night
When some swimmers took flight
And an adequate number survived

In the earliest days of TV
Watching sitcoms filled Billy with glee
He played baseball a lot
After college he taught
But it wasn't his true cup of tea

Doing stand-up routines was his aim
In the finicky show business game
So he took to the stage
For a moderate wage
In pursuance of fortune and fame

Billy later moved west to L.A.
Where he played a young dude who was gay
Earning pretty good dough
On a ground-breaking show
Which in reruns is seen to this day

After that there were offers galore
For roles both at home and offshore
Soon his acting was seen
On the silvery screen
He was rife with artistic rapport

He starred in When Harry Met Sally
In a part that was right up his alley
The film was a hit
For its rhythm and wit
And its splendid romantic finale

City Slickers was truly a blast
With its wonderful story and cast
Where Billy played Mitch
Who was seeking his niche
To atone for his colorless past

Ted Danson

A talented fellow named Danson
Is still breathing, unlike David Janssen
On Cheers he played Sam
Who pursued bearded clam
He was simple, but funny and handsome

In movies Ted's also appeared
And many were stupid and weird
But his role on TV
Drew a six-figure fee
And made him much loved and revered

He appeared in a classic film noir
Body Heat didn't make him a star
But his role in support
As a lawyerly sort
Led to playing a guy with a bar

Sam Malone was the owner of Cheers
Where he served many pretzels and beers
To his weird clientele
With his waitress from hell
Who gave Cliffy and Normy the gears

The show featured Frasier as well
Who dated Diane for a spell
But she yearned for the bone
Of one May Day Malone
When his groin would predictably swell

Three ladies Ted Danson has wed
Also Whoopi once joined him in bed
But that didn't last long
As his average white dong
Didn't hold him in very good stead

Rodney Dangerfield

He never could get no respect
And his wife couldn't make him erect
But his riotous rants
Made us pee in our pants
Rodney Dangerfield had that effect

He was raised in the Borough of Queens
Where he got his first job in his teens
Writing jokes and one-liners
For vaudeville old-timers
To put a few bucks in his jeans

He did stand-up himself after that
With the audience passing the hat
So the guy could get paid
And go out and get laid
But his jokes and his timing were flat

He was known as Jack Roy on the stage
Where he tried to regale and engage
The folks in the crowd
So they'd chuckle out loud
And he'd garner an adequate wage

Rodney left his desired vocation
When he came to the realization
He wasn't that funny
And needed more money
So switched to a new occupation

So aluminum siding he sold
Door to door in the rain and the cold
Getting people to buy
When they didn't know why
After being coerced and cajoled

After nine awful years he returned
To the business for which he had yearned
But he struggled once more
Every joke was a chore
And it made him confused and concerned

So he altered his image and name
To fan his professional flame
Cashing in on his lack
Of societal knack
And abundance of failure and shame

Then the break of a lifetime occurred
After all of the crap he endured
Someone else had got sick
So five minutes of shtick
On the Sullivan Show was procured

All at once, almost fifty years old
Rodney Dangerfield sparkled like gold
With his sudden acclaim
There was riches and fame
With the punches he happily rolled

Rodney died in two thousand and four
Leaving millions of fans wanting more
Of the wonder and mirth
That he brought to this Earth
Where he earned our respect, and much more

Tom DeLay

A fellow called Thomas DeLay
Wielded massive political sway
Until he got caught
Taking bribes quite a lot
To augment his congressional pay

Early on things came easy to Tom
Who delighted his Dad and his Mom
By avoiding the draft
With much deftness and craft
To avoid getting maimed by a bomb

After college he landed a job
Killing pests who ate corn on the cob
And destroyed other crops
Such as barley and hops
Causing farmers to blubber and sob

But real work, Tom believed, was for twits
So he used what would pass for his wits
To get him a seat
With the Texas elite
In the world of the Newts and the Mitts

After Austin Tom thirsted for more
Of the power he'd come to adore
So for Congress he ran
With a definite plan
For much graft and payola to score

For 22 years in D.C.
He made laws for the land of the free
And the home of the brave
Many speeches he gave
And did favors when offered a fee

He made deals that were under the table
In bars over shots of Red Label
Which got him convicted
And rightly depicted
As morally weak and unstable

His verdict was later thrown out
When a judge with significant clout
Reversed the decision
Without inhibition
By finding a reasonable doubt

The case is now pending appeal
As the local D.A. wants to deal
With this matter again
And send Tom to the pen
Which his lawyers will argue with zeal

John Denver

There once was a man known as John
To whom millions of people were drawn
He was brimming with joy
Like a child with a toy
Then one day he was suddenly gone

He was born in a South-western State
With a bit of blond hair on his pate
He sang in a choir
His Dad was a flyer
Who often was rude and irate

In his teens he was hired to play
Local clubs, where the straight and the gay
Went to chat and consort
And drink beer by the quart
Or go out for a puff on a jay

After college young John headed west
To L.A., where he quickly impressed
With his musical skills
Near the Hollywood Hills
Where the starlets are scantily dressed

With his looks and his crisp tenor voice
He made record producers rejoice
From the revenue flow
He was making good dough
And he soon could afford a Rolls Royce

Though he traveled from Sydney to Rome
And from Mexico City to Nome
Playing songs for a fee
With unparalleled glee
Colorado is where he called home

John defended the land and the air
And made millions of people aware
Of the rights and the wrongs
In his speeches and songs
He had values and passion to spare

John Denver was just 54
With a lucrative future in store
And still in his prime
When he ran out of time
Off the breezy Los Angeles shore

Lady Diana

A gal known as Lady Diana
Was a star, much like Carlos Santana
To her smile we were drawn
Then one day she was gone
Now she's resting in peace in nirvana

She was born in to privilege and means
In a nation where people spread beans
Over toast for their tea
As they watch BBC
And they subsidize princes and queens

Diana was shy as a lass
Never showing aggression or brass
But as she matured
She got more self-assured
And developed a beautiful ass

As half of an ill-fated marriage
She often took rides in a carriage
With her hubby named Chuck
Who was rather a schmuck
And was easy to mock and disparage

She gave birth to a couple of lads
Who now live in their own royal pads
One is married to Kate
One is seeking to mate
With nice girls who are keen for his 'nads

She was often seen spreading goodwill
While displaying much passion and skill
In her many crusades
Such as treatment for AIDS
For the millions who can't pay their bill

Lady Di and Prince Charles divorced
After Chuck had successfully sourced
For some sex on the side
Unbeknownst to his bride
Soon a settlement deal was endorsed

Then Diana and Dodi Fayed
Started dating and sharing a bed
Life was treating them well
'Til a driver from hell
Got impaired, then Diana was dead

Cameron Diaz

An actor named Cameron Diaz
Is loaded with style and pizzazz
She's attractive to men
And she gives them a yen
To feel up both the hooters she has

In her first major role in The Mask
She proved to be up to the task
Many tickets would sell
Many manhoods would swell
At the sight of her wonderful ass

After working with comic Jim Carrey
There was something about her as Mary
Once again she was hot
With that butt that she's got
She was funny, like Cheri Oteri

Cameron's still going strong to this day
Though her hair will be soon turning grey
But she still oozes sex
Many men she erects
Even those who are openly gay

Emily Dickinson

In Emily Dickinson's time
Her work didn't earn her a dime
Or a whisper of praise
For the marvellous ways
She excelled with her rhythm and rhyme

She was born in to wealth and excess
And a fancy New England address
She was known to be weird
But she later endeared
With the talent with which she was blessed

With her poetry Emily shone
But very few people were drawn
To the words that she weaved
When she still lived and breathed
Few were published until she was gone

When Emily Dickinson died
The soul of a poet survived
And lives on all around us
To move and astound us
And make us feel better inside

Joe DiMaggio

A once living legend named Joe
Was considered the consummate pro
With his glove and his bat
In his pinstripes and hat
He was talent tied up in a bow

In the 30's Joe signed as a Yank
Whose fortunes had recently sank
There he played 13 years
He had very few peers
And relations with many a skank

He was one of the best at the plate
Hitting safely in 56 straight
He signed up for the war
But he never left shore
They did not want him meeting his fate

Joe had twenty-two hundred base hits
Lifetime average of .326
He made all-star each year
Filling pitchers with fear
In New York they adored him to bits

In the fifties Joe dumped his first spouse
And abandoned their marital house
For a gal named Monroe
And he soon was her beau
He enjoyed what was under her blouse

They got married but later they split
After many a petulant snit
She could charm and allure
And was sexy for sure
Joe enjoyed both her rack and her slit

But with Marilyn Joe reunited
As she still got his unit excited
And they would have re-wed
But the lady got dead
And her killers were ever indicted

Joe was clearly no flash in the pan
He retired a wealthy young man
Near the Florida coast
Where he liked it the most
And caught fish from his catamaran

Later on Mr. Coffee employed him
And to various sites they deployed him
With his smile and his hair
To increase market share
On TV it was hard to avoid him

At age 84 Joe expired
From a nasty disease he acquired
But his image remains
Firmly etched in our brains
As a guy much revered and admired

Celine Dion

A lady we know as Celine
By her fans is considered a queen
She's been here a long time
But she's still in her prime
Like she was as a pimple-faced teen

She was born in trhe land of Quebec
Where a fellow called René Levesque
Once endorsed separation
To start his own nation
The man was a pain in the neck

Celine got her start early on
At home singing many a song
For her friends and her kin
With much vigor and vim
As the pride of her Dad and her Mom

In her native Quebec she became
A gal of some local acclaim
Then her songs got some play
In the U.S. of A.
Which was always her ultimate aim

After that came unbridled success
Nice new clothes and a fancy address
She got rich and well known
For her singular tone
She was loaded with gusto and zest

Now Celine lives in Vegas full-time
And performs at a venue designed
Just for her and her band
Each performance is grand
With much money her pockets are lined

Denny Doherty

Denny Doherty sang like a bird
As millions of people have heard
And still do to this day
Though he's now passed away
From an ailment that couldn't be cured

In a pawn shop he worked early on
But he found himself mightily drawn
To a music career
Long before he'd appear
With a fellow they called Papa John

With The Hepsters young Denny broke in
In the fifties when deejays would spin
Every song they could name
Such as 'Ain't That a Shame'
When a mickey cost less than a fin

In the sixties he sang with a lass
Who later became Mama Cass
With her singular style
And her radiant smile
She was big, both in talent and mass

Then Denny met John and Michelle
And they all got along very well
When they added young Cass
They were cooking with gas
Only not for a very long spell

The Mamas and Papas struck gold
And millions of albums were sold
To a major degree
Denny's voice was the key
To the musical stories they told

Though the group only lasted four years
They were loved by their fans and their peers
For their numerous hits
When our faces had zits
They were music to millions of ears

But Denny had sex with Michelle
When she prompted his unit to swell
Thus began the demise
Of these ladies and guys
Though their records continued to sell

Denny then had a solo career
Which lasted for many a year
On the stage and TV
He was brimming with glee
With a voice we still wanted to hear

Denny Doherty lived out a dream
'Til the day that he ran out of steam
Now he rests in his plot
He is gone, not forgot
Of the crop he was clearly the cream

Kirk Douglas

A wonderful actor named Kirk
Played the friend of a fellow named Earp
In a western locale
At the O.K. Corral
When the Clantons went freaking berserk

He was born to a family of Jews
In New York, where the Knicks always lose
When they take to the court
Often coming up short
As their fans all get wasted on booze

Izzy Demsky is how he was known
When he didn't have hair on his dome
But he took a new name
For the show business game
When his body was totally grown

He found work on the stage early on
But was just an irrelevant pawn
On the theatre scene
Like a young Ben Vereen
Who could dance with the grace of a swan

Kirk was buddies with Lauren Bacall
Who was making a pretty good haul
Making films in L.A.
Near Marina Del Rey
In the era of Charles de Gaulle

So on Lauren's advice he moved west
Where he quickly got work and impressed
With his skill and appearance
And speaking coherence
Which helped him to feather his nest

Pretty soon he was box office gold
And millions of tickets were sold
To cinema buffs
Who relaxed on their duffs
Watching plots of his movies unfold

He made too many pictures to mention
In his fast and amazing ascension
Up the ladder of fame
To substantial acclaim
With no trace of elitist pretension

Robert Duvall

A fellow named Robert Duvall
Has been making a very good haul
On the silvery screen
Like the late Steve McQueen
He's a star from New York to Nepal

San Diego is where he arrived
In the movies is where he has thrived
In a fifty year span
Putting films in the can
He has more than just merely survived

After college he studied his art
In New York where he played his first part
In a Broadway production
Of love and seduction
He learned all his lines off by heart

Pretty soon he was much in demand
For many new films that were planned
With his scope he impressed
As he feathered his nest
Soon a 6-figure fee he'd command

In The Godfather Robert broke through
In a film that was seen as a coup
Where a family of thugs
Killed a peddler of drugs
With a gun that was stashed in the loo

In Network he played a real prick
Who directed a self-serving chick
Who had never been wed
And an old talking head
Who was deemed to be mentally sick

Sheena Easton

Sheena Easton was born one fine day
Long ago in a land faraway
She earned fortune and fame
From her song 'Morning Train'
Which is still getting radio play

Sheena started to sing as a tyke
When her melons had yet to grow ripe
Barbra Streisand enthused her
Her singing infused her
With feelings of blissful delight

After high school she formally trained
In drama and voice, and attained
Much artistic esteem
As she followed her dream
To succeed in the show business game

EMI offered Sheena a deal
Which she took with great gusto and zeal
She soon was a star
With a shiny new car
She was rife with commercial appeal

Pretty soon Sheena's music was known
From Glasgow to London to Rome
And New York to L.A.
In the U.S. of A.
Where she now makes her permanent home

She's been married four times in her life
But has not found success as a wife
Now she's single and free
Just like Bobby McGee
And that Mayberry dude, Barney Fife

Clint Eastwood

A director and actor named Clint
Is well known for his glare and his squint
For his films we're enthused
Now he's old and confused
But he's nearly as rich as The Mint

Clint was born long ago in San Fran
As the son of a steelworker man
He was big as a lad
Like his strapping old Dad
Who lost weight when he sat on the can

In the fifties Clint served in the war
Of Korea, but never left shore
He stayed at Fort Ord
Where munitions were stored
For the purpose of bloodshed and gore

Later Eastwood would meet a director
Who worked in the show business sector
He was very impressed
So arranged for a test
That he'd play on a movie projector

After lessons in acting he'd taken
A pretty good wage he was makin'
He portrayed Rowdy Yates
On the trail with his mates
Herding cattle to bring home the bacon

With a hit TV series behind him
That's when Hollywood wined him and dined him
To play Dirty Harry
Whose tactics were scary
Whose bosses pissed off and maligned him

With his signature line, 'Make my day'
In the signature role he would play
Clint got larger than life
In a scene of great strife
Where he blew many bad guys away

From the 70's up to the present
Clint's been dining on lobster and pheasant
Many women he's wedded
And hundreds he's bedded
His life has been fruitful and pleasant

Clint was offered the role of James Bond
By producers from over the pond
But he turned down the role
As the world's greatest mole
Who humped many a redhead and blond

Many movie awards he has won
Many years he's been named number one
As a box office draw
With his sinewy jaw
And the wile of Attila the Hun

John Edwards

John Edwards had sex with his aide
One of many mistakes that he made
Then the gal had a kid
From the humping they did
So she had to be silenced and paid

But the money he used for this cause
May have broken a couple of laws
They charged him in court
For this dastardly tort
But their case had a number of flaws

His lawyers got John off the hook
But many still think he's a crook
Like a snake in the weeds
For his terrible deeds
His political life is kaput

John Edwards had bailed on his spouse
And their kids and their marital house
She got sick and she died
With her kin at her side
Save for John, who'd turned in to a louse

He was prime for a federal election
And enjoyed much respect and affection
But his plans went awry
With a wandering eye
And a badly misguided erection

Queen Elizabeth

A lady we know as The Queen
Is from Britain, just like Mr. Bean
She's a titular head
Who's been royally bred
To be pompous and stylish and clean

She was born to a world in depression
And a blueprinted line of succession
She grew up in a bubble
To stay out of trouble
At least 'til her royal accession

In the year '52 she was crowned
On a day many Guinness were downed
And she's reigned ever since
With her hubby, the Prince
Who once hunted for fox with a hound

Liz's children are Charles and Anne
Who have never spent time in the can
Chuck was married to Di
But she told him 'bye-bye'
When Camilla made nice with her man

Now the Queen is all wrinkled and grey
But she seems to be doing okay
For an elderly broad
Who does not have a job
And has nothing important to say

Cass Elliot

A lady we called Mama Cass
Was a wonderfully talented lass
She could sing like a lark
But she ate like a shark
You could park a small car on her ass

With the Mamas and Papas she shone
Just like Tony Orlando and Dawn
She went solo as well
Many records she'd sell
But at age 33 she was gone

Many think that she choked on some meat
In the swanky celebrity suite
Of a London hotel
Where she stayed for a spell
Which was home to the rich and elite

But in fact it was due to her heart
Which stopped beating and wouldn't restart
She'd been fasting of late
To cut down on her weight
Which more often than not isn't smart

In the time she was here on this Earth
With her copious talent and girth
And her wonderful smile
She could charm and beguile
Filling millions with gladness and mirth

Peter Falk

As Columbo he charmed us to bits
Winning many a battle of wits
As a slovenly sleuth
Who went searching for truth
With a pencil and pad in his mitts

Peter Falk, who has now gone away
Had a brilliant career in his day
Both in film and TV
In the land of the free
And deserved every dime of his pay

He was born in New York long ago
When America's spirits were low
The markets had crashed
Many hopes had been dashed
And replaced with depression and woe

Peter lost his right eye as a tot
When his iris developed a clot
Underneath his right lid
So they had to get rid
But he never got sad or distraught

After high school he earned a degree
Quite a studious fellow was he
Then he signed for the war
But they showed him the door
When they noticed one eye couldn't see

But acting was always his aim
Not so much for the fortune and fame
But the challenge and fun
Of a yarn nicely spun
And a smidgen of fleeting acclaim

He took courses and landed some parts
And impressed with his timing and smarts
Then on Broadway he played
Decent money he made
He was big in the theatre arts

Soon Hollywood beckoned the man
To go westward and work on his tan
And buy a nice house
As a gift to his spouse
Who was always his number one fan

Peter soon was a bona fide star
With a pool and a shiny new car
On the big and small screen
He stole many a scene
With his charm and his trademark cigar

In his 84th year Peter died
With his daughters and wife by his side
In the time he was here
Many courses he'd steer
And we all went along for the ride

Chris Farley

A talented fellow named Chris
Never knew much contentment or bliss
He was brimming with glee
When on film and TV
But for years there was something amiss

He was born in a Midwestern State
Where they often have cheese on their plate
Chris liked God very much
He was rarely in dutch
Many pizzas and burgers he ate

At Marquette Farley earned a degree
With no clue what he wanted to be
So he worked for his Dad
And he got his own pad
Plus a car and a color TV

Soon a comedy gig was his aim
For the fun and the fortune and fame
So he joined Second City
Where people were witty
And earned much applause and acclaim

Lorne Michaels saw Farley in action
And noted the public's reaction
Chris then joined SNL
Where his coffers would swell
And his acting career got some traction

For five years he earned fame and big money
Life was good and his days were all sunny
While his life off the set
Caused his buddies to fret
On the job he was wickedly funny

Chris made films that were average at best
As both critics and fans would attest
But with Farley on screen
They made plenty of green
He was clearly a master of jest

With his smile he could charm and endear
But one day he no longer was here
His work overjoyed him
But demons destroyed him
In only his 34th year

Mia Farrow

Mia Farrow was born on in L.A.
Where the Angels and Rams used to play
As an actor and wife
She's had gladness and strife
And some issues that won't go away

Mia's parents were show business types
Who'd succeeded in earning their stripes
On the Hollywood scene
So their daughter was keen
To aspire to similar heights

In Peyton Place Mia was cast
In a series that quickly surpassed
Its high expectations
With dramatizations
Of people who lived hard and fast

In Rosemary's Baby she played
A lady in pain and dismayed
That her son was a demon
Produced with some semen
Her husband had never conveyed

In 50 more films she appeared
On the prosperous course that she steered
Seeking fortune and fame
In the film making game
Where she constantly charmed and endeared

Frank Sinatra and Mia were hitched
But Mia would later get ditched
When she wouldn't comply
With the whims of her guy
The divorce left her free and enriched

Andre Previn became Mia's spouse
He was never a jerk or a louse
With their half dozen kids
In their diapers and bibs
They required a very big house

Nine years later they got a divorce
When that marriage had finished its course
Woody Allen then wooed her
And later he screwed her
She liked what he had in his shorts

She and Woody adopted some tots
Then Woody had sexual thoughts
About daughter Soon Yi
When she sat on his knee
And he soon got a case of the hots

What ensued was a nasty estrangement
And for Woody a living arrangement
Which sparked accusations
Of child molestations
Plus copious shock and amazement

To this day there is rancour and hate
And an endlessly running debate
Which began when a dude
Had a thought that was lewd
And his manhood began to inflate

So I offer this tribute to Mia
And toast her with wine or sangria
After all she's been through
Since her Earthly debut
She's still sweeter than Tia Maria

Farrah Fawcett

There once was a lady named Farrah
Who didn't need rouge or mascara
To make her look hot
We adored her a lot
She was foxy, like Tia Ferrera

Corpus Christi is where she was born
Where the summers are humid and warm
In high school she'd blossom
Her beauty was awesome
She could have excelled making porn

Farrah moved to L.A. to pursue
What she always had wanted to do
Seeking fortune and fame
In the show business game
Where she soon made her acting debut

At first she would only appear
In commercials for toothpaste and beer
She was paying her dues
And had nothing to lose
In her quest for an acting career

She married a fellow named Lee
Who played many a role on TV
He was hung like a horse
But they got a divorce
When a judge signed a final decree

Charlie's Angels gave Farrah the chance
Of a lifetime to grow and enhance
Her degree of success
Which she did with finesse
As young men put their hands down their pants

She and Ryan O'Neal had a thing
Farrah never was given a ring
But they did have a kid
From the humping they did
When she still had the world on a string

Later on Farrah's health took a turn
For the worse, raising angst and concern
She bounced back for a spell
And appeared to be well
But her illness would later return

She expired in June of '09
Leaving all of her troubles behind
But her image remains
Etched in millions of brains
As a gal who was one of a kind

Sally Field

There's an actress we call Sally Field
Many virtues and flaws she's revealed
In the roles she has played
Now her hair is all grayed
And her arteries partly congealed

As Gidget she starred on TV
In the role of the late Sandra Dee
She was perky and cute
And she gained some repute
As a gal who was footloose and free

Sally then played a nun who could fly
Though we still haven't figured out why
But it lasted 3 years
Through the gibes and the jeers
Then she found bigger fishes to fry

In the movies her roles were more various
From funny to sad to nefarious
Norma Rae brought her fame
And much Oscar acclaim
And in Punch Line her act was hilarious

In Lincoln she played Mary Todd
Who was kind of a chubby old broad
Whose husband got dead
Due to shots in the head
From a singleton firing squad

Amy Fisher

Amy Fisher, an infamous 'ho
Had a tryst with a loser named Joe
They had sex in his shop
He was old as her pop
But she prompted his manhood to grow

Joey promised he'd split with his spouse
And be more of a man than a mouse
He and Amy would wed
And be out of the red
With the cash from the sale of his house

But this guy, it turned out, was a cad
And he wanted to keep all he had
Like his wife and his bitch
Neither one he would ditch
Making Amy go stark raving mad

So she went to his home packing lead
And she shot Joey's wife in the head
Ripping off half her face
Then away she would race
In the hope that she soon would be dead

But the cops soon caught up with this nut
Who by now was an infamous slut
Looking feeble and frail
She was sentenced to jail
In a case that was open and shut

Joey's wife, Mary Jo, didn't die
Though she lost half her jaw and an eye
She stood by her man
'Til he went to the can
And she learned he was living a lie

Amy later got out on parole
And soon she was selling her soul
Making porn for a fee
And a film for TV
With no virtues at all to extol

Heidi Fleiss

A lady we call Heidi Fleiss
Hired slutty young gals to make nice
With the johns of L.A.
Any time of the day
For a somewhat exorbitant price

Heidi also had worked as a hooker
But she wasn't that good of a looker
So she hired some skanks
But it caused her much angst
When the vice squad decided to book 'er

She served 20 months in the can
For the prostitute ring that she ran
So that rich horny guys
With their brains in their flies
Could get laid, then go work on their tan

It was rumored a young Charlie Sheen
Was a fellow who often was keen
To have sex for a fee
With great gusto and glee
As a part of his normal routine

But Heidi refused to divulge
All the names of the men who'd indulge
In hot sex at her place
Thus avoiding disgrace
For those fellas who sported a bulge

Larry Flynt

A colorful fellow called Larry
Has always been somewhat contrary
He publishes smut
Showing many a slut
Whom for years have been missing their cherry

He's been vilified, censured and shot
For the ethics and standards he's got
Dirty needs he's fulfilled
Once he nearly got killed
All his models get ogled a lot

Once he published a funny cartoon
Just to needle, debase and lampoon
Jerry Falwell, a preacher
And anti free speecher
Who croaked not a minute too soon

Falwell sued but was beaten in court
As he couldn't establish a tort
Mr. Flynt won the day
So did not have to pay
It was ruled what he printed was sport

Larry thinks that the world is uptight
So he flaunts its conventions for spite
With much zeal and elan
Just to show that he can
It fulfills him with joy and delight

In March, nineteen seventy-eight
Larry Flynt nearly met with his fate
When a sniper took aim
Not to wing or to maim
But to make him go join Sharon Tate

Since that day Larry sits in a chair
Often fraught with much pain and despair
Lots of grief he's endured
And his diction is slurred
But he's lucid and fully aware

Henry Fonda

There once was a fellow named Fonda
Who was known from L.A. to Rwanda
For the roles he portrayed
In the movies he made
Such as Fail-Safe and On Golden Ponda

He was born with no hair on his pate
Long ago in a Midwestern State
Where the farmers grow corn
When the weather is warm
And raise cows to be eaten as steak

After college he took to the stage
Often working for minimum wage
Then he moved to L.A.
And decided to stay
Where he later would die of old age

In the 30's he landed some parts
In the field of the cinema arts
He impressed with his skill
And put cash in the till
And had sex with a bevy of tarts

Then came fifty spectacular years
Inducing both laughter and tears
With his singular gift
To divert and uplift
He was loved by his fans and his peers

In Twelve Angry Men he was great
In a story of passion and hate
As a man in defiance
Of blinkard compliance
He more than just carried his weight

Mister Roberts provided a role
As a fellow pursuing the goal
Of maintaining morale
In a war time locale
When his captain was losing control

Henry Fonda was married a lot
Six times he was tying the knot
Seven children he had
He was not a great Dad
With depression he often was fraught

But in spite of his angst and his woe
He worked hard and made plenty of dough
In the time he was here
Filling millions with cheer
He was always the consummate pro

In the year '82 Henry died
With Peter and Jane by his side
And his wife Shirlee Mae
At his home in L.A
After truly a wonderful ride

'Tennessee' Ernie Ford

There once was a fellow called Ernie
Who sang many songs on his journey
He was troubled, but great
'Til he met with his fate
And they took him away on a gurney

His parents were Clarence and Maud
Who believed in the power of God
Whose word they obeyed
Gospel music they played
They were happy as peas in a pod

Ernie studied in classical song
And his voice got remarkably strong
Then with other draftees
He was sent overseas
When the Second World War came along

In the war he dropped bombs from a plane
Inflicting much anguish and pain
On his targeted prey
In a land faraway
As great ships fought it out on the main

Then he worked at a radio station
But it wasn't his chosen vocation
So he went on the road
Where much talent he showed
As a baritone singing sensation

When a record executive heard him
Ernie's vocals and showmanship spurred him
To offer a deal
With a lot of appeal
Of a chance for success he assured him

Nearly 60 LPs he recorded
And with stardom and cash was rewarded
Ernie Ford was revered
On TV he appeared
With respect he was widely accorded

Ernie struggled a lot with the booze
Since the time he was paying his dues
On the road every week
Social comfort he'd seek
So he'd go to the bar for a schmooze

At age 72 Ernie passed
When his liver just ran out of gas
In his time on this Earth
He filled millions with mirth
And with liquor filled many a glass

Joe Frazier

A fellow they called Smokin' Joe
In his time battled many a foe
Beating men of great bulk
To a blood spattered pulp
When he fought in the ring toe to toe

He was born in a deep southern State
Where he often had grits on his plate
His family was poor
Life was hard to endure
But his will to survive was innate

With his Dad he watched fights on TV
And decided he wanted to be
A boxer one day
For the fame and the pay
Like a guy called Muhammad Ali

Joe left home at the age of fifteen
To excel on the prizefighting scene
Though his Mom disapproved
Off to Philly he moved
To be trained as a punching machine

A man named Yank Durham saw Joe
And he proved to be much in the know
In the boxing profession
Where speed and aggression
Could garner a shitload of dough

Joe rose up through the ranks undefeated
And then for his country competed
In the Tokyo Games
Where he scrambled some brains
Donning gold when his bouts were completed

Later, back in the States as a pro
He made many more rivals eat crow
Then Ali got the shaft
For denouncing the draft
Causing years of unspeakable woe

That's when Joe got the heavyweight crown
And was quickly a man of renown
And the pick of the pack
But Ali would come back
And call Frazier a thick-headed clown

What ensued were three fights for the ages
Well covered in all the sports pages
Joe lost two out of three
To the brilliant Ali
But he earned many millions in wages

Joe passed on in his 68th year
And millions of fans shed a tear
For a man of great style
With a lovable smile
Who put many a man on his rear

Sigmund Freud

There once was a fellow named Freud
Who was smart, quite unlike Woody Boyd
Who amused us on Cheers
Serving cocktails and beers
Which Cliff Clavin and Normie enjoyed

Sigmund Freud was a shrink by profession
Hearing many a tawdry confession
He was Austrian born
Long before we had porn
To relieve us from angst and depression

As the 'Father of Psychopathology'
He embraced a unique ideology
Where the patients he treated
With brain cells depleted
Exposed their psychotic chronology

He often made use of cocaine
When he suffered his own mental pain
He thought sex was the source
Of much gloom and remorse
And he also enjoyed Mary Jane

Freud's been dead now for two generations
But in various manifestations
He's still part of our lore
That we cannot ignore
And still cited in long dissertations

This verse is a tribute to 'Siggy'
Who was known as an erudite biggie
Who believed every guy
Yearned to unzip the fly
Of his Mom and have sex with her giggy

Jerry Garcia

A fellow called Jerry Garcia
In the sixties conceived an idea
To establish a band
With a singular brand
And be known from L.A. to Korea

Early on he was musically keen
He was fed rock and roll as a teen
Chuck Berry enthused him
His antics amused him
He longed to be part of the scene

As a student he wasn't too bright
Much less likely to study than fight
Many classed he skipped
And he often got ripped
Which fulfilled him with boozy delight

His parents once made him enlist
In the army, and Jerry was pissed
So he drank and he sassed
So his stint didn't last
After many a slap on the wrist

He set out to develop his skills
On guitar, and get stoned to the gills
With some like-minded chums
Who were living like bums
And performing in cheap bar and grills

It was obvious Jerry could write
So the boys all decided one night
To establish a band
That would travel the land
And quite often get high as a kite

They performed for a pittance of bread
Just enough to buy gas and get fed
Then a record exec
Gave Garcia a cheque
Thus began the regime of 'The Dead'

Jerry's era was not without pain
But for more than three decades he'd reign
With his talent and quirks
He enjoyed all the perks
Which included his friend, Mary Jane

Jerry struggled with demons a bit
But he gave us the joy of his wit
And his singular style
That would soothe and beguile
In his life many reefers he lit

Prematurely our hero would pass
Like James Dean and the late Mama Cass
But his music remains
Very stuck in our brains
Still a perfect enhancement for grass

Marvin Gaye

A man that we called Marvin Gaye
Didn't live to out-welcome his stay
In a moment of madness
That filled us with sadness
A bullet took Marvin away

He was born and brought up in D.C.
Where they govern the land of the free
Early on in his life
There was copious strife
And a shortage of laughter and glee

Marvin hit the proverbial road
As a teen, when he thought he'd explode
If he stayed near his Dad
So he got his own pad
In a faraway area code

He always had wanted to sing
For the fortune and fame it could bring
So he joined The Marquees
Who were totally pleased
After taking him under their wing

With The Moonglows he later appeared
On the musical path that he steered
Berry Gordy was jazzed
By their skill and pizzazz
And the loudness with which they were cheered

In Detroit, as a singer and drummer
He was seen as a bright up-and-comer
Soon he starred on his own
With his singular tone
But his personal life was a bummer

There were demons that plagued Mr. Gaye
That he never was able to slay
To escape from his pain
He got hooked on cocaine
Like a lot of great stars of his day

In his lifetime of 44 years
Through a gamut of blood, sweat and tears
Marvin Gaye stole our hearts
With his songs on the charts
And was loved by his fans and his peers

Mel Gibson

A Hollywood actor named Mel
In his brain has burned many a cell
He has talent for sure
And can charm and allure
But he's also the boyfriend from hell

He was born long ago in New York
When a baby was brought by a stork
To his mother and dad
Who were joyful and glad
Unaware he'd turn in to a dork

To Australia the Gibsons would go
Where ridiculous animals grow
That's where Mel found his niche
And developed an itch
To get in to the business of show

Through the years he became very rich
But his life has had many a glitch
From substance addiction
To courtroom conviction
To calling his girlfriend a witch

Mel has ranted some dastardly views
While impaired after binging on booze
He was publicly bashed
And his image was trashed
When he blamed every war on the Jews

John Gotti

There once was a fellow named Gotti
Who often behaved rather naughty
Many people he killed
In the role he fulfilled
As a boss in the mob luminati

In The Bronx he was born long ago
Where his folks didn't have enough dough
To give him nice things
Like a sandbox or swings
Or a quarter to go to the show

John was part of a gang as a teen
Where he learned to be part of a team
With a goal to defeat
Other punks on the street
With a fist or a kick to the spleen

He soon earned a big reputation
Through many a rough altercation
Where he beat on his foes
From their heads to their toes
Which infused him with joy and elation

In his 20's he joined the Gambinos
Got married and raised some bambinos
He rose up through the ranks
Spreading terror and angst
To the Irish, the Blacks and Latinos

The eighties brought John much success
And his enemies lots of distress
In a big double cross
Gotti murdered his boss
Then summarily changed his address

In his neighborhood John was a hero
Like Joe Pesci or Robert Di Niro
Many charges against him
Annoyed and incensed him
But total convictions were zero

John used Sammy Gravano, a cat
Who could help with a gun or a bat
When he needed some muscle
To help in a tussle
But then he turned in to a rat

The feds, with Gravano's assistance
Encountered much legal resistance
But they sent Dapper Don
Off to jail as a con
Where he lived out his wretched existence

Hugh Grant

A splendid young actor named Hugh
Late one evening had nothing to do
Back in June '95
So he went for a drive
Then he noticed his manhood had grew

He encountered a lady named Brown
And asked if she'd like to go down
And make nice with his meat
From his passenger seat
To bring joy to his night on the town

But their deal never came to fruition
And his chubby went in to remission
When the cops came along
And threw ice on his dong
As reported on Inside Edition

Hugh Grant would get past all this strife
To resume his remarkable life
As an actor of note
With a vigorous scrote
Who got bored having sex with his wife

But apart from one goofy faux pas
He's still a great box office draw
Much wealth he's acquired
He's widely admired
And witty, like George Bernard Shaw

Lorne Greene

There once was an actor named Lorne
From the town where Paul Anka was born
We all saw him as 'Ben'
Reading books in his den
With a fire to keep himself warm

He arrived back in 1915
When the movies were silent and clean
He grew handsome and strong
And before very long
He found work on the radio scene

He left his Canadian land
For an acting career that he planned
Which would make him a star
With a shiny a new car
And a house that cost many a grand

Lorne got parts in some films and TV
Playing extras that no one would see
But he got his big break
And was soon eating steak
When Bonanza went on NBC

The show was a hit from the start
Every actor was good at his part
Michael Landon played Joe
Much wild oats he would sow
With many a ravishing tart

Pernell Roberts played Adam for years
Mending fences and rounding up steers
But after six seasons
For various reasons
He yearned for a change of careers

Dan Blocker, as Hoss, was quite big
He could snap a small tree like a twig
He was strong as an ox
Needed custom-made socks
In saloons many beers he could swig

But Lorne Greene, playing Ben, was the best
In his sideburns and big barrel chest
He fought evil and won
With his fists and his gun
And looked cool in his brown studded vest

As Ben Cartwright he gave us much pleasure
Sunday nights in our evenings of leisure
So we honor Lorne Greene
Who was great on the screen
A uniquely Canadian treasure

Larry Hagman

A wonderful actor called Larry
Is almost as old as Chuck Berry
J.R. Ewing he played
Who quite often got laid
And relieved many gal of her cherry

Larry's mother once played Peter Pan
And her son was her number one fan
He began his career
In his 21st year
When he oozed lots of verve and elan

He would later be cast as a meanie
But first there was I Dream of Jeannie
Where he got his first break
And good money he'd make
In the role that he played as a wienie

Then along came a series called Dallas
That featured a guy full of malice
And the riches of oil
That was drilled from the soil
By a family that lived in a palace

As J.R. Larry Hagman would shine
As a man who had crude to refine
And a wife to betray
Played by Miss Linda Gray
Who would often be hammered on wine

Brother Bobby fought hard with J.R.
Tooth and nail, at their ranch or a bar
Bob took after his Mother
And hated his brother
Their battles left many a scar

But J.R. could outfox all his foes
Who were never as quick on their toes
As this splendid conniver
Who left no survivor
And often got naked with hoes

Larry Hagman is now dead and gone
But his spirit and image live on
In reruns we see
Late at night on TV
In our hearts he will always belong

Tom Hanks

A fellow we know as Tom Hanks
As an actor rose up through the ranks
And turned in to a star
Now he drives a nice car
And has money in numerous banks

Tom was born near the city of 'Frisco
Up north from San Luis Obispo
He grew up in the age
Of the great Jimmy Page
And survived through the era of disco

As a teen he was very religious
Before he got strong and prodigious
For the films he has made
And the men he's portrayed
The awards he has won are prestigious

His first major role was in Splash
And it made him a star in a flash
In Big he was cute
Like Jane Fonda in Klute
Who gave many a client a rash

In Apollo 13 he appeared
In a role where his character feared
Getting burned to the bone
As he dropped like a stone
When he didn't, the audience cheered

You've Got Mail was a tale of romance
And a story of taking a chance
Where two people on-line
Started taking a shine
Until one got a bulge in his pants

In A League of Their Own Tom Portrayed
A coach who had not made the grade
Who had got in to dutch
Due to boozing and such
So his nerves were decidedly frayed

In Cast Away Tom was alone
And could not call his wife on the phone
Or have sex with her crotch
It was painful to watch
When he slept on a mattress of stone

But he also made movies that stunk
That should have been tossed in the dump
Such as Turner and Hooch
Where he worked with a pooch
Also Dragnet was no Forrest Gump

Huntz Hall

A great comic actor Huntz Hall
Played a guy with not much on the ball
As a Bowery Boy
He provided much joy
As the silliest one of them all

He was born when they had no TV
In New York, in the land of the free
Back when radio shows
Gave us cause to repose
Even though there was nothing to see

As a child he performed on the air
And displayed a theatrical flair
Then on Broadway he played
Where more money he made
Not too far from The Met and Times Square

But one role Gave Huntz Hall his repute
As a quirky and silly galoot
In his playing of 'Satch'
Many schemes he would hatch
That were always more daft than astute

As small children we played with our toys
As we filled all our households with noise
But more quiet we'd be
When our little TV
Showed the films of The Bowery Boys

Slip Mahoney was boss of this crew
Though he didn't have much of a clue
Whitey, Bobby and Chuck
Very often were struck
By his fist, just for something to do

At Louie's the boys would hang out
Where the soda would spew from a spout
Wen catastrophe loomed
They would nearly be doomed
By some rotten, unscrupulous lout

But the boys saved the day every time
As they battled with masters of crime
With their numbered routines
In a borough near Queens
And their brains lacking reason and rhyme

Huntz passed on in his 80th year
And we're glad for the time he was here
As Satch he amused us
Regaled and enthused us
And caused us to smile ear to ear

Oliver Hardy

There once was a fellow named Ollie
Who was tubby, and hence very jolly
In films he amused us
His antics enthused us
His life was devoted to folly

He was born in a deep southern State
With nary a hair on his pate
His family picked cotton
Before it went rotten
And always had food on their plate

He broke in to the show business sector
When hired to run a projector
The movies enthralled him
Soon destiny called him
Like music once summoned Phil Spector

He earned roles in some terrible flicks
In the time of Mae West and Tom Mix
When he met up with Stan
They came up with a plan
To create a few comedy pics

As Laurel and Hardy they thrived
With the riotous tales they contrived
For twenty-five years
Earning kudos and cheers
For much fun and diversion they strived

More than one hundred movies they made
As they rose to the top of their trade
They performed for a King
In the nation of Sting
And for that they were royally paid

But the reaper of death would arrive
For Ollie at age 65
He was great in his time
With his partner in crime
When they both were alert and alive

Prime Minister Stephen Harper

He was born and grew up in Toronto
Where Rob Ford has been known to get blotto
On booze and cocaine
'Til he's feeling no pain
And he can't find the keys to his auto

To Alberta he moved as a teen
To work on a drilling machine
For Imperial Oil
Who rummage the soil
As part of their daily routine

Stephen studied and earned a degree
Then worked for his local MP
To keep him elected
And soon was connected
To numerous powers that be

Then he ran for a seat of his own
And spent many days on the phone
Collecting support
And did not come up short
Much political savvy was shown

In the 90s he worked for Reform
To change what was seen as the norm
In the way things were run
And before he was done
He'd be taking his party by storm

The year was two thousand and six
When the liberals were acting like pricks
So the people got even
By voting for Stephen
Paul Martin's regime hit the bricks

Under Harper the nation did well
And seemed to come out of her shell
But the honeymoon ended
When Stephen defended
Bad moves by his own personnel

With his glibness and lies wearing thin
Every day he gets under the skin
Of a lot of canucks
Who believe he's a putz
With a permanent vacuous grin

Woody Harrelson

His first major role was in Cheers
As a yokel who served many beers
To Normie and Clavin
The bar was a haven
To them and their booze swilling peers

Woody Boyd was naive and obtuse
And slow witted like Bullwinkle Moose
A breath of fresh air
Who had flowing blond hair
And a tight little farm boy caboose

As Woody he made us all laugh
As a server on Sam Malone's staff
Who was awkward and shy
With a glint in his eye
In a series delightfully daft

After Cheers Woody Harrelson played
Many wonderful roles and was paid
More and more for his work
As a brazen young Turk
Like Tom Cruise or a young Dennis Quaid

He portrayed Larry Flynt and was splendid
As a guy both attacked and defended
For publishing smut
And for being a nut
Which is what he had always intended

In White Men Can't Jump he was funny
And the movie made plenty of money
But Money Train stunk
Like a freshly killed skunk
Who wasn't as quick as a bunny

But most of his films have done well
As his bank account started to swell
He portrayed Mickey Knox
And he blew off our socks
As a murderous boyfriend from hell

In real life Woody's frank and outspoken
He believes they should legalize tokin'
He eats like a vegan
He drinks like a pagan
And thinks that his government's broken

He believes 9/11 was staged
By the White House so war could be waged
A commission held court
But their work came up short
So his doubts still have not been assuaged

Gary Hart

A man that we call Gary Hart
Was regarded as clever and smart
Silver-tongued and astute
And quite handsome to boot
He had politics down to an art

Then his dong got aroused by a tart
And Gary decided to start
An illicit affair
With his wife unaware
He was dining on Rice a la carte

Soon some nosy reporters were prying
And many a rumor was flying
But Gary denied them
The press, he defied them
To prove through his teeth he was lying

Those reporters quite gladly complied
And on Gary they constantly spied
Soon the fling was exposed
And a chapter was closed
Gary's run for the White House had died

So again a potential big cheese
Was dishonored and brought to his knees
Through a meaningless tryst
He was hung out to twist
In the fickle political breeze

Gary Hart is politically through
But he's still finding plenty to do
Now he writes and he speaks
But no office he seeks
And by only his wife he gets blew

Phil Hartman

A comedy genius named Phil
Never made it to over the hill
He was shot by his wife
Who then took her own life
Years ago, and we're missing him still

Phil Hartman was born a canuck
But never would fire a puck
He grew up in the States
Where he first went on dates
And pulled many a prank for a yuck

After working in graphic design
He found himself taking a shine
To performing in skits
Getting by on his wits
Many skills he was keen to refine

With a group called The Groundlings he trained
Where an instinct for humor he gained
As he honed all his skills
Close to Beverly Hills
Major stardom would soon be attained

SNL was in ratings remission
So Lorne Michaels gave Phil an audition
He stayed for eight years
And impressed all his peers
With many a comic rendition

On NewsRadio Phil had a part
In a show that was stylish and smart
With the world at his feet
He was rich and elite
Like he wanted to be from the start

But one horrible night in L.A.
Mr. Hartman was taken away
In a moment of madness
We still feel the sadness
He's missed very much to this day

Hugh Hefner

A horny old fellow called Hef
Gets his meals from his personal chef
Lots of money he's made
He gets frequently laid
And politically leans to the left

In Chicago Hugh Hefner was born
And he once was a subject of scorn
When he first published pics
Of some bare naked chicks
He was charged with distributing porn

After college he worked writing ads
With some other young ladies and lads
For a men's magazine
Which was stylish and clean
For the cool university grads

One day Hefner demanded a raise
As his work was engendering praise
His request was denied
And he took it in stride
But there soon was a parting of ways

He somehow came up with 10 grand
For a new magazine that he planned
With provocative mixtures
Of stories and pictures
Of many a mammary gland

Hefner soon was a publishing king
With a mansion where people could swing
While surrounded by cooze
And imbibing on booze
Like Champagne or a Singapore Sling

Paris Hilton

A gorgeous young gal known as Paris
Is prone to upset and embarrass
Her Mom and her Dad
When she poses unclad
Or gets caught driving drunk in her Yaris

To the Hilton estate she's the heiress
And already a rich millionairess
Her best friend is Nicole
To get laid is their goal
They're both straight, unlike Neil Patrick Harris

She's attractive, like Tony Bandaras
She enjoys getting smashed on her terrace
She has cash in the bank
Just like Hilary Swank
Many men want to probe her clitaris

Her Dad's a big wheel, like the Ferris
She's a bit of a flake, like Chuck Barris
She's outlasted her stay
But she won't go away
'Til she's dead, like the late Roger Maris

Benny Hinn

A scammer they call Benny Hinn
Gets the desperate and thick to send in
Many millions in dough
When their spirits are low
Then he takes his new Jag for a spin

In Israel Benny arrived
As a baby his parents contrived
To Toronto they moved
Where their lives were improved
As a child he was never deprived

As a teen he became a fanatic
For beliefs that were strange and dogmatic
Religion enthused him
The Bible suffused him
He yearned to become charismatic

He moved to the U.S. of A.
Where he really began making hay
He did some research
Then the founded a church
Which he runs in a fraudulent way

Benny claims he's an agent of God
And a man all the world should applaud
For healing the ill
With miraculous skill
In The States and in nations abroad

But Benny has many a critic
Who know he can't help the arthritic
Or the deaf or the blind
As his pockets are lined
He is nothing if not parasitic

Alfred Hitchcock

There once was a man known as Hitch
Who early in life found his niche
Making movies galore
Full of terror and gore
And it made him both famous and rich

Sir Alfred was born in Great Britain
Where allegiance to queens is befittin'
There he made 26
Unremarkable flicks
But his story had yet to be written

At age 40 he moved to L.A.
Made one film and decided to stay
To direct many more
That we've come to adore
Like when birds hunted humans as prey

In Psycho he scared us to bits
When a woman got covered with slits
In his scene in a bath
Of a lunatic's wrath
With a big kitchen knife in his mitts

Rear Window got packed with suspense
When a man was observing events
In his neighbors' abodes
Using various modes
In the end it got very intense

And then there was North by Northwest
Which clearly was one of his best
Where Eva and Cary
Had dinner with sherry
Then later had sex when undressed

Now it's been many years since he passed
Leaving all the great works he amassed
That we still love to watch
As we sip on a scotch
But they seem to be over too fast

Jimmy Hoffa

Jimmy Hoffa was born in the State
That features the Mackinaw Strait
In Detroit he was reared
Where the man disappeared
And presumably met with his fate

In his youth he got very involved
With unions, which later evolved
In to powerful factions
With shady transactions
And murders that couldn't be solved

With The Teamsters he served and ascended
To senior positions, which ended
When Jimmy got jailed
From a caper that failed
And his freedoms and rights were suspended

After seven long years in a cell
Being guarded by armed personnel
Richard Nixon stepped in
And forgave him his sin
Then himself got in dutch for a spell

When back on the streets Jimmy sought
Reinstatement that couldn't be bought
Then in '75
He went out for a drive
And was grabbed in a kidnapping plot

No one living knows what happened then
On a mid-summer's day way back when
But it's safe to assume
That he met with his doom
At the hands of some very bad men

Dustin Hoffman

An actor we call Dustin Hoffman
Is a Jew like the late Andy Kaufman
Many stories he's told
Now he's wrinkled and old
So in bed he is likely a soft man

In 'The Graduate' Hoffman broke through
As Ben Braddock, who hadn't a clue
He was boring and staid
And he'd never got laid
Till his neighbor began pitching woo

But his character wanted her daughter
Who was younger and smarter and hotter
With a nicer caboose
Soon all hell would break loose
And his sanity started to totter

Katherine Ross played the girl from next door
Miss Ann Bancroft the wrinkled old whore
Who was patently nuts
For one horny young putz
'Sounds of Silence' would highlight the score

In the end things worked out pretty well
With the young'uns both happy as hell
And the skank from next door
Would have sex never more
As her hubby no longer would swell

In the following years Dustin's flicks
Are a heterogeneous mix
Of provocative roles
That are good for our souls
When we need a vicarious fix

J. Edgar Hoover

There once was a fellow named Hoover
Who was known as a shaker and mover
On the Washington scene
He was sneaky and mean
And an infamous power abuser

He was born long ago in D.C.
The home of the powers that be
Where he lived all his life
And did not take a wife
But quite often dressed up as a she

After law school he landed a job
Fighting commies, unrest and the mob
Then he rose up the ranks
By protecting his flanks
And was soon living high on the hog

For decades he served as Director
Of the government crime fighting sector
At The Bureau he reigned
Too much power he gained
As the ultimate data collector

Many Presidents wanted to fire
This man who was hard to admire
But he knew too much dirt
He could use to subvert
Their prestige if they made him retire

Howard Hughes

The man that we called Howard Hughes
Once was profiled a lot in the news
Many courses he steered
He was wealthy but weird
And distrusted the blacks and the Jews

He was born back in 1905
And was bigger than life when alive
Even dead he's compelling
His books are still selling
Though one was made up and contrived

Half of Vegas he owned at one time
In the heyday of organized crime
Many women he'd woo
He bought studios too
And an airline when still in his prime

Lovely starlets he often romanced
In the hopes he'd get in to their pants
And quite often he scored
His testosterone soared
As the front of his trousers advanced

Many think Howard Hughes was connected
To the mob, who got people elected
So they'd be in their debt
Then big favors they'd get
With their assets corruptly protected

At one time there were rumors galore
That his mind wasn't working no more
He was manic depressive
And super obsessive
And flaky, like Zsa Zsa Gabor

Later on it was clear he was nuts
There were truly no ifs, ands or buts
Many brain cells were dead
He would not leave his bed
His associates hated his guts

Then in '76 Howard died
As a man who had lost all his pride
He had cash in the bank
But no gas in the tank
And no family or friends by his side

In his time he had fortune and fame
And no shortage of sadness and pain
He followed his heart
And was strikingly smart
When he still had full use of his brain

Saddam Hussein

There once was a man called Saddam
Who was driven to go on the lam
When troops were deployed
And his land was destroyed
By that beacon of peace, Uncle Sam

He was born in the town of Tikrit
And grew up to be rich and elite
And mean and sadistic
And opportunistic
While practicing fraud and deceit

But his rise to the top of the heap
Wasn't easy and didn't come cheap
He was exiled and jailed
Long before he was hailed
By a nation of terrified sheep

In the 80s he started a war
With Iran, causing bloodshed galore
Ronald Reagan helped out
With his militant clout
In an effort to settle a score

Saddam then invaded Kuwait
A timid but affluent state
But George Bush number one
Went and spoiled his fun
And his men beat a hasty escape

Later Bush number two was elected
And claimed there were weapons detected
When he lied through his teeth
As Commander-in-Chief
And conventions of war were rejected

Saddam got arrested and tried
Then was hung by his neck 'til he died
Now he's deep in the ground
So we're all safe and sound
He's no longer a thorn in our side

Michael Jackson

The once King of Pop Michael Jackson
Owned a ranch where he'd go for relaxin'
Many Grammys he won
He had surgeries done
So he'd look like a white Anglo-Saxon

It was rumored that Mike was abused
By his father, and often was bruised
By this parent from hell
If he didn't sing well
And it left him in tears and confused

Michael somehow survived the disdain
From his Dad, who was likely insane
Finding wealth and success
Out of sadness and stress
But he carried some permanent pain

He recorded an album called 'Thriller'
With a lot of great tunes and no filler
He invented a walk
He performed for his flock
Who regarded their man as a pillar

He got married to Lisa Marie
They believed it would fill them with glee
She looked hot in a thong
But it didn't last long
When she learned he was hung like a flea

Through the years there were facial mutations
And he faced one or two accusations
That he fought and denied
Though they put him off stride
On the first he would make reparations

Michael went on the lam for a while
But was planning a comeback in style
When he suddenly passed
Now he's peaceful at last
But his music still earns him a pile

Samuel L. Jackson

A fellow named Samuel L. Jackson
Has earned plenty of box office traction
And artistic acclaim
In the show business game
That can match any white Anglo Saxon

He grew up in the Volunteer State
Where they often have grits on their plate
His old man hit the bricks
When young Samuel was six
He was known as a bit of a snake

Samuel majored in drama at school
To prepare for a trade that is cruel
And fraught with rejection
And chronic depression
But also like, totally cool

After college he landed some parts
On Broadway and stole a few hearts
With his presence and skill
He put cash in the till
His producers were jazzed by his smarts

Nasty demons then entered his brain
Causing chronic addiction and pain
And almost his career
From the liquor and beer
And a habit of snorting cocaine

But in rehab he cleaned up his act
With his liver and mind still intact
Then when things got okay
He moved west to L.A.
Where the babes are synthetically stacked

After that came unbridled success
Lots of cash and a fancy address
And a shiny new car
Much befitting a star
Who'd emerged from the depths of distress

In Goodfellas Jackson played Stacks
Who was killed in a series of whacks
In True Romance he croaked
With much blood he was soaked
Which the public enjoyed to the max

And then he played Jules in Pulp Fiction
With wonderful violence and diction
Jackie Brown was a blast
With a wonderful cast
That was based on a smuggling conviction

Sam's been married for numerous years
Unlike most of his Hollywood peers
Who switch spouses like socks
While they're switching their locks
With replacements they purchase at Sears

Steve Jobs

There once was a man known as Steve
Who had many great tricks up his sleeve
He earned billions in pay
But was taken away
Far too soon, just like Christopher Reeve

As a youth it was patently clear
That the course he was destined to steer
Would involve innovation
And visualization
Each day of each calendar year

In the world of computers he shone
Many talented people were drawn
To his digital knack
He gave birth to the Mac
One of many great products he spawned

There was nothing the man wouldn't try
When expanding his piece of the pie
He was great at PR
And a media star
And the Apple of many an eye

Steve expired while still in his prime
When he tragically ran out of time
But his legend remains
And his vision sustains
In a way that is pure and sublime

Billy Joel

A musical genius named Billy
Has endured, unlike Milli Vanilli
As a great balladeer
He has filled us with cheer
Now he's verging on over the hilly

He was born in The Bronx on this date
Long ago in the Empire State
Where he lives to this day
Earning plenty of pay
When his concerts do well at the gate

His father was classically trained
On piano, which Billy disdained
But later embraced
When it suited his taste
And propelled him to fortune and fame

When The Beatles appeared on TV
Billy knew that he wanted to be
Singing songs on a stage
For a sizable wage
This new music consumed him with glee

With The Echoes he made his debut
In the business he chose to pursue
Thus began a career
Lasting many a year
Earning many a glowing review

On Piano Man Billy contrived
A wonderful album that thrived
On the charts of the day
With much radio play
From that disc many more were derived

The Stranger scored big on the charts
Showing off Billy's song writing smarts
An Innocent Man
From New York to Spokane
Is still great as the sum of its parts

Billy battled depression for years
Once his life nearly ended in tears
But he somehow endured
As he grew and matured
With the help of his friends and his peers

Michael Jordan

There's a fellow we knew as Air Jordan
Years ago many planes he was boardin'
When he left his abode
To play games on the road
His career was supremely rewardin'

With the Bulls he was clearly the leader
With three kids, he was also a breeder
He could jump really high
That's no word of a lie
Off the court he was quite the good deeder

In his prime he won titles galore
And controlled what went down on the floor
He got pounded each night
But he always took flight
He was graceful as Eva Gabor

Once he tried playing baseball, but stunk
As he couldn't hit pitches with junk
Also those that had none
So it wasn't as fun
As a drive through the paint for a dunk

He's enjoyed spending time on the links
And he plays quite a lot, but he stinks
He has lost many bets
And incurred many debts
But his wife still wears diamonds and minks

After failing at 2 other sports
He returned to the basketball courts
Where he starred once again
Making boys out of men
Faking many right out of their shorts

Andy Kaufman

Andy Kaufman was one of a kind
With his wondrous, maniacal mind
In his time on this Earth
We were charmed by his mirth
And the fact he would not be confined

He was born in New York one fine day
And later he moved to L.A.
Where he followed his dream
'Til he ran out of steam
And at age 35 passed away

He was never a teller of jokes
With the image such humor evokes
He preferred naughty pranks
Causing worry and angst
Or a strange diabolical hoax

On Taxi, as Latka, he charmed us
His manner amused and disarmed us
But quite often on stage
He'd go in to a rage
And by creepy design he alarmed us

Andy lived in a different dimension
Where he captured our hearts and attention
With his wit and his wile
And his singular style
Unencumbered by fluff and pretension

Harvey Keitel

A fellow named Harvey Keitel
Is Jewish, like Howard Cosell
For the movies he's made
He's been handsomely paid
In the land of the Liberty Bell

He quit school at the age of sixteen
And signed up to become a Marine
Then he served overseas
Where they speak Lebanese
When a Communist threat was foreseen

When Harvey returned to New York
He recorded procedures in court
And auditioned for parts
In the theater arts
Where at first all his efforts fell short

He persisted in chasing his dream
And soon he was making the scene
After many auditions
In Broadway renditions
And later the silvery screen

Harvey landed a role in Mean Streets
And impressed with his acting techniques
The film was a hit
With its boldness and grit
Drawing copious glowing critiques

In The Border Keitel played the lead
In a tale of corruption and greed
On the Texas frontier
Where the raising of steer
Can fulfill a carnivorous need

In Reservoir Dogs he portrayed
A man who had morally strayed
Who was lured and enticed
To be in on a heist
As a part of a killing brigade

He also appeared in Pulp Fiction
A movie with wonderful diction
And multiple plots
Earning numerous props
As a film that defied all description

Grace Kelly

An actress we knew as Grace Kelly
Was a fox from her face to her belly
Right on down to her pubes
And her wonderful boobs
She caused many a manhood to swelly

Early on she had roles on TV
And she filled all the sponsors with glee
As they padded their books
From her talent and looks
She was hot, like the late Sandra Dee

But it's movies that made her a star
Like Liz Taylor and Hedy Lamarr
She was rich ever since
She got wed to a prince
Then one day took a drive in his car

It's believed that she suffered a stroke
Crashed the car, then she never awoke
After many long years
Still she charms and endears
And still chubbifies many a bloke

John F. Kennedy

A fellow we call JFK
Did many great things in his day
His friends called him Jack
He was sharp as a tack
But too soon he was taken away

He was born in a town by the sea
As a part of a family tree
That was rooted in cash
He had charm and panache
Like John Wayne or Mohamed Ali

After college John fought in the war
Shooting enemy soldiers galore
Then for Congress he ran
With a big-hearted plan
To assist the oppressed and the poor

In the Senate he later would serve
With much energy, wisdom and verve
Then when Ike left his job
John's old man and the mob
Called in favors they'd held in reserve

JFK sought the White House and won
Beating Nixon, who sweated a ton
Papa Joe helped him out
With his cash and his clout
Which he gladly endowed to his son

While in office he made an impression
And sometimes a moral transgression
When he strayed from his wife
Causing marital strife
Which the press never bothered addressin'

He faced Khrushchev and caused him to blink
When those men took the world to the brink
Of a nuclear war
And unspeakable gore
Driving millions of people to drink

The Peace Corps was Kennedy driven
Where food and assistance were given
To nations in need
That had millions to feed
Who could not make an adequate livin'

Civil rights was a critical topic
That this President deemed patriotic
So he wrote some new laws
In support of a cause
Where The Congress had long been myopic

Jack was held in quite lofty regard
But his time in The White House was marred
By his secretive flings
In L.A. and Palm Springs
Where his public persona was scarred

Bay of Pigs was his signature blunder
Where his men tried to pillage and plunder
The nation of Cuba
Just north of Aruba
But all of his plans went asunder

But to most JFK was a saint
Who governed with poise and restraint
But could also be tough
When the going got rough
And on camera be folksy and quaint

John F. Kennedy never would see
If a second four years was to be
In a murderous plot
He was fatally shot
On this day long ago in Big D

The Warren Commission reported
That Kennedy's life was aborted
By a singular man
With a dastardly plan
But some facts were ignored or distorted

Now many long years have gone by
Since we said an untimely good-bye
To a man of great hope
And unlimited scope
But it still isn't clear as to why

Ted Kennedy

A rich politician named Ted
Had demons inside of his head
Many drinks he could chug
His old man was a thug
Once he left a young lady for dead

Teddy's parents were Rosie and Joe
Who had lots of connections and dough
Joe had dubious friends
Who were means to his ends
As they helped him to prosper and grow

Ted had really a nice head of hair
And a sister who wasn't all there
So they screwed with her brain
With malignant disdain
As they thought it would end her despair

He had brothers named Bobby and John
In the 60's they both would be gone
So the profits of war
Could continue to soar
With the death and destruction they'd spawn

One night Teddy got in to a jam
And he had to spend time on the lam
When the car that he drove
Ended up in a cove
And the senator opted to scram

He abandoned his friend in the water
And he swam off to shore like an otter
Then he got a hotel
And laid low for a spell
As a mother and dad lost their daughter

Ted never served time in the clink
And was soon very much in the pink
He went on with his life
And made peace with his wife
With a shiny new car and a mink

Mark Knopfler

Dire Straits was a band for the ages
Who evolved through some wonderful stages
With a player named Mark
Who provided the spark
They took home quite a shitload of wages

With a song called The Sultans of Swing
They would score a resounding ka-ching
And with Mark on guitar
Playing eight to the bar
To the heights of success they would spring

Later on Mark would go on his own
With the singular rhythm and tone
In his magical hands
Found in no other bands
Both his range and his fandom have grown

With his soul and his fingers he thrills
All the young and the over the hills
We are moved by his gift
When we're needing a lift
Or have trouble with paying our bills

Now Mark Knopfler is old as can be
But still on his game and on key
And he still makes us smile
With his talent and style
But more often he has to go pee

Diana Krall

A talented lady named Krall
Is a star from New York to Nepal
With her fingers and pipes
She has earned all her stripes
People buy her CDs at the mall

She's married to Elvis Costello
Who now is more thoughtful and mellow
Than he was in his youth
Now he's long in the tooth
Like that Scotsman who sang Mellow Yellow

Diana was born in BC
Where she played the piano for free
At the age of fifteen
On the speakeasy scene
But she now gets a 6-figure fee

To develop her natural skill
And the dream she was keen to fulfill
East to Boston she'd go
Saving oodles of dough
As a scholarship footed the bill

After that she was off to L.A.
Where many a venue she'd play
With her singular flair
And her flowing blond hair
She was soon making serious hay

Her first album was called Stepping Out
And erased any possible doubt
That this gal was a star
Just like Hedy Lamarr
And those bozos who sang Twist and Shout

What's ensued is a brilliant career
And a penchant to charm and endear
To the genre of jazz
She brings style and pizzazz
And she's always a pleasure to hear

Stan Laurel

A comical fellow named Stan
Was loaded with verve and elan
He charmed and beguiled
Like an innocent child
And was more than a flash in the pan

Stan was born in the land of Great Britain
Where millions are openly smitten
With chips and warm beer
That they make disappear
And where bowing to queens is befittin'

In his twenties he crossed the Atlantic
To a land far away and gigantic
Where movies were made
And where actors got paid
To be funny or mean or romantic

In the States he met Oliver Hardy
A splendidly fat tub of lardy
They weren't close right away
But they later made hay
As a team, much like Coke and Bacardi

Stan and Ollie made movies and dough
At a time of foreclosures and woe
When the world was depressed
And in need of some jest
To the movies they always could go

John Lennon

There once was a fellow named John
To whom millions of people were drawn
For his passion and smarts
He put joy in our hearts
Then quite sadly, too soon he was gone

In Liverpool Lennon was reared
Back when Churchill was loved and revered
For his wisdom and grit
And his singular wit
On the course he so capably steered

John's childhood was less than ideal
As his songs later on would reveal
His old man was a rake
And his Mom was a flake
So the household was far from genteel

His uncle and aunt took him in
Where a healthier time would begin
He was prone to rebel
But they treated him well
When he needed a circle of kin

In college they forced him to leave
After many a lucky reprieve
So to music he turned
Where he always had yearned
To find out what his mind could achieve

With The Quarrymen John had a hoot
And found out he was very astute
Writing songs for the band
As they traveled the land
Playing venues of shallow repute

Paul and George joined the band later on
But the drummer they had wasn't strong
He was able but bland
So he had to be canned
Then a man known as Starr came along

As The Beatles the boys struck it rich
With rarely a lapse or a glitch
They invaded The States
And had steak on their plates
They had clearly discovered their niche

When the band had enough of the life
That was causing them anguish and strife
And too many a snit
They decided to split
And to many it cut like a knife

John and Yoko found plenty to do
Such as writing and hoisting a few
With their well-to-do friends
Who were setters of trends
In the musical world that they knew

John was basking in semi-retirement
With nary a missing requirement
When a nut shot him dead
With a gun full of lead
Near his luxury condo environment

Though the time that we knew him was brief
We can cling to his basic belief
If we give peace a chance
All our world will enhance
Both in times of great comfort and grief

David Letterman

A funny old bugger named Dave
Is known in the home of the brave
And the land of the free
As a noted emcee
And a splendidly mischievous knave

He was born in the Hoosier State
Where they often have corn on their plate
His old man ran a store
Selling flowers galore
David's childhood was calm and sedate

In college he went on the air
Making students and others aware
Of the news of the day
For a pittance of pay
While displaying a whimsical flair

Later on he moved west to L.A.
To develop his show biz cachet
On the comedy scene
With a stand-up routine
Where the Angels and Rams used to play

NBC soon got wind of his knack
For delivering many a crack
Drawing laughs and guffaws
And much noisy applause
They believed he was sharp as a tack

So the network gave David a shot
On a show every morning which got
Many glowing reviews
But it failed to enthuse
Many viewers or sponsors a lot

The program was cancelled, but then
Dave was given a job once again
In a much later slot
He was suddenly hot
Like Madonna, who married Sean Penn

Later David felt totally snubbed
When a plan to promote him was scrubbed
So he left NBC
And his lucrative fee
He was clearly resentful and bugged

CBS scooped him up in a trice
And paid him a walloping price
For services rendered
Great work he's engendered
His hair now is whiter than rice

Dave's announced he'll retire next year
All his fans will be shedding a tear
When he walks off the stage
To begin a new page
Of a truly amazing career

Jerry Lee Lewis

A fellow they call Jerry Lee
Filled record producers with glee
When his albums struck gold
Many millions were sold
In the earliest days of TV

He was born in The Pelican State
Where his manhood would later inflate
When his cousin dropped in
And although she was kin
They decided to go on a date

As a child Jerry sang all the time
Back when smokes could be bought for a dime
He was almost prodigious
His folks were religious
And thought unwed sex was a crime

But Jerry made up his own rules
He believed those who didn't were fools
He did what he wanted
And never was daunted
His hands and his voice were his tools

After high school he traveled around
To see what good gigs could be found
But they mostly were bad
For this pipe dreaming lad
As he worked on perfecting his sound

After playing in many a dive
The break of his life would arrive
With a single audition
A dream reached fruition
And soon a new car he would drive

Sun Records gave Lewis his chance
To put a few bucks in his pants
With a studio stint
He'd no longer be skint
And his stagnant career could advance

Soon fortune and fame reared its head
Jerry Lee bought a sumptuous spread
And suits by the dozen
Then married his cousin
And humped her each night in his bed

Six more ladies he married since then
Who serviced his infinite yen
For multiple mates
Of all sizes and weights
Like Madonna once serviced Sean Penn

A movie called Great Balls of Fire
Showed the times of a man we admire
Who followed his gut
And pinched many a butt
Since the days when he sang in a choir

Abraham Lincoln

There once was a fellow named Abe
Who lived 'til the day he was slayed
John Wilkes Booth took his life
As he sat with his wife
Who was visibly shocked and dismayed

In Kentucky Abe Lincoln was born
A State that would later be torn
When a war was declared
And a nation prepared
For a lot of dead soldiers to mourn

He moved to the Hoosier State
Where they always have corn on their plate
In the law he was trained
Much respect he attained
Winning many a rousing debate

In The Senate he later would serve
With copious gusto and verve
Then The White House he sought
Which he won by a lot
But many down south were unnerved

As President, Lincoln decided
That the law of the land was misguided
And that slaves should be freed
But the south disagreed
And the country was badly divided

What ensued was a horrible war
Full of death and destruction galore
The battles were heated
The south was defeated
But one aimed to settle the score

Now one hundred and forty-nine years
Have elapsed since his family and peers
Put Abe Lincoln to rest
In a hickory chest
With their faces all covered in tears

On the penny and five-dollar bill
Lincoln's image is used to instill
A sense of assurance
And fiscal endurance
Cashiers keep them locked in a till

Abe Lincoln was clearly a man
Who was never a flash in the pan
With his odd looking beard
He was loved and revered
But was not a big hit with the Klan

George 'Goober' Lindsey

He played one major role in his life
As a buddy of Taylor and Fife
In a deep southern town
Of no special renown
In a show full of comical strife

As Goober, a pumper of gas
He never could get any ass
He was shy with the gals
So hung out with his pals
Such as Otis and Ernest T. Bass

George Lindsey was born in a State
Where they often have grits on their plate
And the weather is mild
He loved sports as a child
And had many a lovable trait

After college he opted to go
To New York to be taught by a pro
How to play out a role
In pursuit of his goal
To be acting for oodles of dough

After that he moved west to L.A.
Finding very few roles he could play
So he struggled a while
Then he played Goober Pyle
And his problems all melted away

Lindsey died in his 84th year
But in reruns we see him appear
With Barney and Andy
And Emmett, who's handy
And Floyd, played by Howard McNear

Rich Little

A talented fellow named Rich
Early on found his show business niche
With his skillful impressions
And facial expressions
He's one funny son of a bitch

Mr. Little was born a canuck
Where the chances for eminence suck
So he moved to L.A.
And decided to stay
In pursuit of the almighty buck

He's done thousands of shows through the years
And delighted his fans and his peers
With his vocalizations
In numerous nations
He constantly charms and endears

Now he's basking in semi-retirement
In the sinful Las Vegas environment
Where he's snugly ensconced
There is little he wants
Good clean fun is his only requirement

In Vegas he's still playing live
He continues to comically thrive
As he contemplates life
With his friends and his wife
And Viagra enhancing his drive

Kenny Loggins

Kenny Loggins was born in the State
Where the Mariners step to the plate
With his pal Jim Messina
In many arena
They did very well at the gate

Second Helping was Kenny's debut
In the business he chose to pursue
Which was singing on stage
For a meaningful wage
And despoiling a groupie or two

Messina and Ken got together
And found out they were birds of a feather
So they drafted a plan
And quite soon they began
A successful recording endeavor

Five years later they opted to split
After cranking out hit after hit
On the rock and roll charts
Stealing millions of hearts
And their fans didn't like it a bit

Kenny started a solo career
And continued to charm and endear
Both on albums and live
He did more than survive
Earning plenty of cash every year

On soundtracks he also has shone
Many glowing reviews he has drawn
For his Caddyshack theme
He earned plenty of green
Like Bill Murray, who tended the lawn

Jim Messina and Ken reunited
In two thousand and five and incited
Excitement galore
Fans were shouting for more
Many bongs full of pot were ignited

Vince Lombardi

An NFL legend named Vince
In Green Bay was a virtual prince
Once he guided the Pack
Often blowing his stack
No one's matched him for excellence since

He was born in New York long ago
Where the Hudson and East Rivers flow
Vince's father sold meat
To the poor and elite
At a time when employment was low

Becoming a priest was his goal
Much religion was etched in his soul
But he gave up the call
For a chance to play ball
Then move on to a mentoring role

After high school he studied at Fordham
When the college agreed to accord him
A scholarship deal
For its fiscal appeal
But the classes consumed him with boredom

After college Vince knew in his heart
That he'd never be given a part
Playing ball with the pros
So that chapter would close
But another was ready to start

To the coaching profession he went
And began an impressive ascent
To fame and success
And a fancy address
Which was how he believed it was meant

For the Giants he worked for a while
And developed a singular style
And strategic approach
As a thinking man's coach
Who was known for his wit and his guile

Then the job of his lifetime arrived
When an offer to Vince was contrived
To coach in Green Bay
For more power and pay
And for nine splendid seasons he thrived

Five championships Vince would amass
While combining the run and the pass
With a stingy defense
Who were fast and immense
For the kicking of serious ass

The Super Bowl Trophy is named
After Vince, who is widely acclaimed
As the pick of the pack
Who was sharp as a tack
And is now in his sport's Hall of Fame

Sophia Loren

In the city of Rome she was born
At the time when her country was torn
By the Second World War
With its carnage and gore
Which left millions both dead and forlorn

As a youngster she oozed sensuality
With her face and unbridled vitality
Her massive torpedoes
Caused heightened libidos
In men with a randy mentality

Sophia began her career
And the course she was anxious to steer
In pursuit of her goal
With a meaningless role
That she played in her 17th year

In the fifties she polished her skills
And was able to pay all her bills
With the money she made
For the roles that she played
Prompting many vicarious thrills

Sophia would soon be a star
Like Clark Gable and Hedy Lamarr
Very much in demand
Earning hundreds of grand
With a mansion and shiny new car

She's made 94 movies in all
And also a pretty good haul
In kudos and cash
As a box office smash
She's prolific, like Robert Duvall

Norm Macdonald

Norm Macdonald was born one fine day
In the year that they shot JFK
He loves to perform
He's Canadian born
But resides in the U.S. of A.

Early on he wrote scripts for Roseanne
Where a gal with a hubby named Dan
Spouted venom and bile
To amuse and beguile
In her highly dysfunctional clan

Norm did stand-up routines to amuse
Many patrons in bars swilling booze
To forget all their woes
He was quick on his toes
As he went about paying his dues

Just for Laughs gave Macdonald his chance
To impress with his comedy rants
At a very young age
On a national stage
Where they laughed 'til they peed in their pants

In the 90's he joined SNL
And his bank account started to swell
His uncanny impressions
And goofy digressions
Were great 'til his final farewell

Norm was fired for not being funny
By a guy who was clearly a dummy
He was given the boot
By a jerk in a suit
Leaving millions of fans feeling crummy

But Macdonald would land on his feet
And soon he was rife and replete
With offers of parts
In the comedy arts
Where he still was consdered elite

In numerous films he appeared
And each one was decidedly weird
Most were critically panned
Or dismissed out of hand
But some copious profits were cleared

Norm has also returned to his roots
Providing much laughter and hoots
To his fans who stuck by
This hilarious guy
Through his many comedic pursuits

Madonna

A lady we know as Madonna
Was born not too far from Toronna
She was great in her youth
Now she's long in the tooth
And a star from New York to Botswana

She arrived in the Wolverine State
With a lot of dark hair on her pate
She would later go blond
Scanty outfits she donned
Causing many young men to inflate

In high school she started to dance
In ballet for the joy and romance
The rhythmic gyrations
Would earn her laudations
And also a scholarship chance

But she dropped out of college to go
To New York where her talent would grow
And her bank account too
From the things she could do
But she wasn't the star of the show

Madonna then altered her plans
And sang in some rock and roll bands
Once again she impressed
Often scantily dressed
Showing off both her mammary glands

She later set out on her own
And even more talent was shown
Soon a record deal came
Then much money and fame
From the various seeds she had sown

She cranked out the hits fast and furious
Her life was no longer penurious
She drove a nice car
She was truly a star
With a lifestyle quite plush and luxurious

By now many millions of men
Were rating Madonna a '10'
On their horniness scale
As a great piece of tail
But she only had eyes for Sean Penn

She was married to Sean a few years
While amazing her fans and her peers
With her trailblazing ways
Drawing critical praise
And a lot of libidinous leers

She married Guy Ritchie as well
After casting her sexual spell
By exposing her rack
And her vaginal crack
Thereby causing his member to swell

Now Madonna is footloose and free
Still dancing and singing on-key
As the queen of soft porn
Many hats she has worn
In a lifetime of wonder and glee

Mickey Mantle

A Yankee we knew as The Mick
When on base was remarkably quick
With his bat he was great
From both sides of the plate
Of the pack he was clearly the pick

Mickey felt from the time he was small
He was put on this Earth to play ball
So he practiced each day
And blew coaches away
Long before he grew up big and tall

After high school he played in the minors
Where he hit many homers and liners
And learned how to cuss
As he traveled by bus
And ate meals in the crummiest diners

Two years later he went to the show
Where he played with the great Joltin' Joe
18 years after that
Mickey hung up his hat
And retired with plenty of dough

More than 500 homers he hit
And saved many a game with his mitt
He won championship rings
Had occasional flings
And admitted he often got lit

On the field he did everything well
There was nowhere he didn't excel
But he drank like a souse
And behaved like a louse
He was often the husband from hell

A liver replacement he got
As the one he was using was shot
Two months later he died
With his wife at his side
And his many transgressions forgot

Steve Martin

An accomplished performer named Steve
Is skilled like you wouldn't believe
From his stand-up routine
To the silvery screen
He's made all of us laugh 'til we heave

He was born in the 40's in Texas
Where George Bush drives a bullet-proof Lexus
And where State executions
Are seen as solutions
Which never has failed to perplex us

As a youngster Steve moved to L.A.
Where the Dodgers would soon go to play
Where his realtor Dad
Was a bit of a cad
And Rock Hudson was secretly gay

After high school to college he'd mosey
To major in drama and poesy
Soon the acting bug bit
When he showcased his wit
It was clear that his future was rosy

Philosophy also enthused him
Its platitudes somewhat amused him
And helped him compose
In the business he chose
As his craving for humor perfused him

Steve would drop out of school to pursue
The thing that he most liked to do
Which was making a buck
Giving people a yuck
While they guzzled a drinky or two

He also had jobs writing jokes
For some music and comedy blokes
Such as Tom and Dick Smothers
Glen Campbell and others
When sponsors were makers of smokes

But on stage is where Steve made his name
Paving nicely his highway to fame
With his cockeyed approach
Many subjects he'd broach
To much laughter and raving acclaim

Then Hollywood beckoned for Steve
To see if he'd try to achieve
On the screen like the stage
For a much higher wage
If he still had some tricks up his sleeve

Through the following years he amassed
A body of work that has passed
Every critical test
Both in drama and jest
Now his cash and his assets are vast

In The Man with Two Brains he was goofy
In Dead Men Don't Wear Plaid he was spoofy
In Roxanne he had woes
And an over-sized nose
Doing stand-up he brought down the roofy

Now Steve's doing the thing he likes best
With much musical skill he is blessed
So he travels the land
With the Steep Canyon band
And their concerts have always impressed

John McEnroe

A fellow they call Johnny Mac
For his antics took plenty of flak
He was great at his sport
When he played on the court
And got Tatum O'Neal on her back

In Germany Johnny was born
A land that was brutally torn
In the Second World War
When our boys went ashore
Shooting Nazis with malice and scorn

His family moved back to The States
Where they always had food on their plates
And a shiny new car
After Dad passed the bar
John was cool so got plenty of dates

At 8 years of age John began
Playing tennis and soon had a plan
To be ranked number one
By the time he was done
And retire a very rich man

He took lessons to learn every shot
And to know what he oughtn't and ought
To do when he played
And improve at his trade
So he'd win much more often than not

John developed a masterful game
On his journey to fortune and fame
He turned pro at nineteen
And although he was green
Pretty soon all the world knew his name

In singles and doubles he's won
Every tournament under the sun
Now he's semi-retired
And widely admired
And still playing tennis for fun

Howard McNear

A fellow named Howard McNear
Played a barber for many a year
With a singular flair
And with only one chair
In a town with no whiskey or beer

He was born back in 1905
Back when acting was only done live
On the stage he was skilled
In the roles he fulfilled
In the age of the Jitterbug Jive

He did radio too in those days
When he wasn't performing in plays
Then in movies he played
Where more money he made
Earning copious kudos and praise

In his time he played numerous parts
But the one that stole all of our hearts
Was a man who cut hair
Every week on the air
And was blessed with more kindness than smarts

His shop was a Mayberry hub
In a town that did not have a pub
With his friends killing time
Barney Fife fighting crime
And Miss Crump giving Andy a chub

Floyd gave haircuts to Andy and Ope
And to Goober, a bit of a dope
Otis Campbell dropped in
Always stinking of gin
And in need of Lavoris or Scope

Bette Midler

A gal we refer to as Bette
Has the look of a randy coquette
And a radiant smile
That can charm and beguile
She's a star from L.A. to Tibet

After high school she majored in drama
In the State where a guy named Obama
Insists he arrived
As a baby contrived
When his Papa had sex with his Mama

Bette moved to New York to audition
For many a Broadway rendition
And made an impression
Her style was refreshin'
A dream soon would come to fruition

Barry Manilow called her 'Divine'
After critically taking a shine
To her style and her sound
Which would soon be renowned
Like the famous and late Patsy Cline

Since that time when she broke on the scene
Bette Midler's earned plenty of green
From her records and such
We've enjoyed her so much
To her fans she's revered as a queen

Dennis Miller

A man that we call Dennis Miller
Is alive, quite unlike Phyllis Diller
With his glibness and wits
People love him to bits
In the comedy world he's a pillar

As a journalist Dennis was trained
But then his priorities changed
When on local TV
He became an emcee
Just as if it was all pre-ordained

Later on in his stand-up routine
He enjoyed being rude and obscene
And began making hay
With his sharp repartee
Like a guy all hopped up on caffeine

Lorne Michaels saw Dennis's act
And it made him get totally jacked
As he chuckled out loud
Like the rest of the crowd
At the Comedy Store, which was packed

Michaels signed him to join SNL
Where the ratings had recently fell
And he soon was a star
With a shiny new car
And humped many a mademoiselle

Six years later he had his own show
Cracking wise for a shitload of dough
Then won Emmys galore
Not unlike Dinah Shore
When he bolted and joined HBO

On Monday Night Football he stunk
Even though he exhibited spunk
And his singular wit
But he just didn't fit
So the ratings and audience shrunk

Then on Fox and on CNBC
Dennis worked as a funny emcee
Now he works when he chooses
And still he amuses
When paid a significant fee

Roger Miller

The man who sang King of the Road
Was raised in a modest abode
But later got rich
With his lyrics and pitch
After many wild oats had been sowed

He grew up in southwest Oklahoma
Where he earned him a high school diploma
In Korea he fought
Several commies he shot
As the napalm gave off an aroma

To Nashville he later would go
Where musicians made serious dough
But things didn't go well
So he quit for a spell
As his confidence level was low

To music he later returned
Where he once was summarily spurned
Music City embraced him
The media chased him
For stories and photos they yearned

With 'Dang Me' and then 'Chug-a-Lug'
Roger soon was financially snug
But his personal life
Soon was riddled with strife
As he battled his craving for drug

In his time many kudos he drew
As his universality grew
He created great mirth
In his time on this Earth
And he wished us a Do Wacka Do

Liza Minnelli

A lady called Liza Minnelli
Was a singer, like Gino Vannelli
And an actor as well
Much like Barbara Mandrell
She was known from New York to New Delhi

Liza's parents were Judy and Vince
Who lived like a princess and prince
On their western estate
Very plush and ornate
Back when lighters were loaded with flints

She started to sing as a tyke
And learned she could charm and delight
With her talent and style
And her radiant smile
In the city of glamor and hype

Liza moved to New York as a teen
And performed on the speakeasy scene
And on Broadway as well
Where she worked for a spell
And got hitched to a guy who's a queen

After that she made records galore
And played concerts at home and offshore
Getting rich and well known
From Manhattan to Rome
Leaving galleries shouting for more

In the movies she also excelled
In a lofty regard she was held
For the roles she portrayed
She was very well paid
As her ego and bank account swelled

She's been wed several times in her life
But each time there was marital strife
All her men came and went
By collective consent
Now she's glad to be nobody's wife

Liza's battled with demons for years
And is known by her kin and her peers
As a regular boozer
And Valium abuser
Through decades of blood, sweat and tears

Joni Mitchell

A musical goddess named Joni
From the nation of Brian Mulroney
Has a singular style
And she's made quite a pile
For herself and the people at Sony

Early on she worked clubs and cafés
In the midst of the rock and roll craze
But her genre was folk
So she mostly was broke
While the radio played Purple Haze

Joni often performed on the street
When she hungered for something to eat
Earning nickels and dimes
With the jugglers and mimes
In the rain and the snow and the sleet

But her music could not be ignored
And she soon would be headed toward
Much commercial success
And a fancy address
That she earlier couldn't afford

Many wonderful tunes she has sung us
Many wonderful lyrics she's brung us
Over so many years
Both her fans and her peers
Are so thankful this lady's among us

Marilyn Monroe

Early on she was called Norma Jeane
Then was known on the silvery screen
By the name of Monroe
Making plenty of dough
With her penchant for stealing a scene

For acting this gal had a flair
And a style that was quirky and rare
She could charm and beguile
With her radiant smile
But she often was fraught with despair

With a sexual glitter she shone
To her humor and charm we were drawn
Many lovers she had
She was flaky a tad
Far too soon we would color her 'gone'

Now it's fifty long years since she died
With no family or friends at her side
But the why and the how
Are unknown even now
And for many the tears haven't dried

Keith Moon

A rock & roll drummer named Moon
In the seventies left us too soon
He was just thirty-two
When his gig was all through
In his time he was mad as a loon

He was just seventeen when The Who
Were a talented group that was new
When their drummer got canned
Mr. Moon joined the band
Then a lot of white powder he blew

On the drums he could blow you away
And still can, on CDs, to this day
He was magic on stage
In a wonderful age
We would marvel at how he could play

Keith attempted to cure his affliction
And abandon his life of addiction
To the booze and cocaine
That had addled his brain
But he lacked the sufficient conviction

In September of seventy eight
Moon went out with his gal on a date
Paul McCartney was there
At a swanky affair
He appeared to be calm and sedate

But next morning Keith Moon would be dead
Filling millions with sadness and dread
He took pills and passed on
Now his anguish is gone
Like the demons that lived in his head

Dudley Moore

A fellow we called Dudley Moore
Was a guy we all came to adore
With his charm and his cuteness
And comic astuteness
He left all his fans wanting more

He was born with club feet and endured
Being teased and maliciously slurred
By his classmates at school
Who were nasty and cruel
Lots of sadness and crying occurred

In music young Dudley excelled
And in lofty esteem he was held
When he played for a crowd
Both his parents were proud
As his talent and confidence swelled

But music was not the vocation
That filled him with joy and elation
So he went for auditions
For acting positions
In many a manifestation

With his natural comedy flair
Dudley often was seen on the air
Drawing major guffaws
And effusive applause
He had wit and charisma to spare

Then he packed up and moved to L.A.
In the movies he wanted to play
On the silvery screen
Not unlike Steve McQueen
And Rock Hudson before he was gay

With Bo Derek, in '10', he was great
As a guy who was yearning to date
A foxy young lass
With a wonderful ass
You could serve as a meal on a plate

In Arthur he guzzled much booze
And often threw up on his shoes
In a wonderful flick
That was stylish and slick
And got nothing but glowing reviews

In Unfaithfully Yours he portrayed
A composer whose lady had strayed
But his planned retribution
Was fraught with confusion
This movie should not have been made

Dudley died in two thousand and two
Leaving all of his fans feeling blue
We enjoyed his great wit
He was one funny Brit
He had humor right up the wazoo

Mary Tyler Moore

A comedy legend named Mary
Was a neighbour of Millie and Jerry
Then she worked for Lou Grant
Who had sex with her aunt
Who was often abrupt and contrary

Laura Petrie she came to be known
As a gal who was incident prone
With a husband named Rob
Who wrote jokes for a job
And a son from the seed he had sown

In the sixties for 5 splendid years
Rob and Laura drew kudos and cheers
As a guy and his wife
Who's the love of his life
And in reruns the show still appears

Mary Richards then burst on the scene
As a gal who was morally clean
And as cute as can be
As she filled us with glee
She was held in the highest esteem

With Gordy and Murray and Ted
She didn't make very much bread
While producing the news
As her boss guzzled booze
And her dates tried to get her in bed

Rick Moranis

A comedy actor named Rick
Got his start doing radio shtick
Then at SCTV
For a nominal fee
He earned laughs with his wonderful wit

He was born in the town of Toronto
Where the Mayor gets totally blotto
On booze and cocaine
'Til he's feeling no pain
Then inhales a big plate of risotto

At SCTV he fine-tuned
His talent which quickly ballooned
His great imitations
Were comic sensations
As many a star was lampooned

He then made his movie debut
In the silly cult classic, Strange Brew
Then in Ghostbusters Rick
Played a guy who was thick
Earning many a glowing review

In Parenthood Rick played a dude
Whose marital life comes unglued
The film was adored
He received an award
Then more lucrative offers ensued

Rick is semi-retired these days
Having gone through a difficult phase
When his wife passed away
There was sadness each day
From their premature parting of ways

Jim Morrison

In the 40's a genius was born
Who always refused to conform
For his lack of politeness
He showed no contriteness
And earned both affection and scorn

Jim Morrison did what he wanted
And often he brazenly flaunted
The rules of convention
With roguish dissension
He couldn't be muzzled or daunted

He was born in a Florida town
Where the hurricanes often blow down
What stands in their way
As the locals all pray
That no livestock or people will drown

San Diego, not long after that
Was where Jim would be hanging his hat
And began to compose
Many poems and prose
He thought writing was where it was at

He studied at UCLA
For a job making movies one day
But the booze and cocaine
And the sweet Mary Jane
Were too tempting and got in his way

But his passion for writing remained
And would not be subdued or constrained
Then he met some musicians
With growing ambitions
And soon he was vocally trained

A book called The Doors of Perception
Gave Jim and the boys a conception
Soon they played as The Doors
And had records in stores
With promoters they made a connection

They got famous almost overnight
And they often got high as a kite
But with Morrison's vision
And cutting derision
Their future looked wealthy and bright

'Break on Through' hit the charts early on
Later 'People Are Strange' came along
There were many more hits
And we loved them to bits
As we puffed on a joint or a bong

But Jim wasn't good at reality
And all of its rigid banality
He had much on his plate
But he seldom was straight
He was losing his mind and vitality

As his life spiraled out of control
Nasty habits were taking their toll
On a man with a gift
Who was clearly adrift
And had demons corrupting his soul

Back in '71 Jimmy died
With no one at all by his side
But his image remains
In our hearts and our brains
As a modern day Jekyll and Hyde

Eddie Murphy

Eddie Murphy was born in the State
Where the Rangers and Islanders skate
In pursuit of a puck
And a shot at the Cup
In the city that's always awake

Eddie's Dad was a casual comic
In clubs serving vodka and tonic
His Ma worked for Bell
With its vast clientele
When computers were still embryonic

He began doing funny routines
For his buddies while still in his teens
He enjoyed Richard Pryor
Who later caught fire
Destroying his shirt and his jeans

In the 80's Lorne Michaels engaged
Eddie Murphy to work on his stage
Where he stole every scene
Not unlike Ben Vereen
He got rich at a very young age

SNL was the gig that began
A stand-up career that would span
Many lucrative years
Then he shifted careers
He was clearly no flash in the pan

To Hollywood Eddie would go
Where he netted a shitload of dough
Making movies galore
Both at home and offshore
As he reached his artistic plateau

In 48 Hours he played
Reggie Hammond, a wise cracking spade
Who helped out a cop
On his neighborhood block
Where illegal transactions were made

Axel Foley was maybe the best
Of his roles, where he truly impressed
With his natural skills
Set in Beverly Hills
As millions of fans would attest

The Nutty Professor was great
He had numerous parts on his plate
His tale of romance
Made us pee in our pants
And expanded his massive estate

Ogden Nash

There once was a man known as Nash
Who made a voluminous splash
With the way that he wrote
As a poet of note
At the time of the stock market crash

In 1902 he arrived
Back when cars were exclusively drived
Down the road or the street
By the rich and elite
Who were rarely, if ever, deprived

In his twenties he started to write
And found out he could please and delight
With the words that he chose
For his poesy and prose
Which he often was asked to recite

Fourteen books Ogden penned in his time
Mostly verses of organized rhyme
Plus prosaic bon mots
About life and its throes
From the daft to the smart and sublime

As a writer the man was a pro
Though he never made very much dough
But he stuck to his guns
With his wonderful puns
'Til a man put a tag on his toe

Rick Nelson

A matinee idol called Rick
Was a magnet to many a chick
Who were keen for his dong
He sang many a song
As he played his guitar with a pick

In New Jersey Rick Nelson arrived
As a baby his parents contrived
But it's sad to report
That his life was cut short
In a plane crash that no one survived

He played Ricky in Ozzie and Harriet
When Ben-Hur rode around in a chariot
Back when Wally and Beave
Were too cute to believe
And Roy Rogers did tricks with a lariat

When the acting bug didn't take hold
A new chapter began to unfold
Rick could carry a tune
Causing groupies to swoon
And was soon turning vinyl to gold

Rick enjoyed many wonderful years
And removed many ladies' brassieres
He had demons as well
He was under their spell
But was loved by his fans and his peers

In 'Poor Little Fool' he regaled us
In 'Travellin' Man' he availed us
Of his casual style
Which could charm and beguile
'Garden Party' was good for what ailed us

Ricky Nelson was gone in a flash
And entombed in a mountain of ash
When the plane he was in
Went in to a spin
On its way to a horrible crash

Jack Nicholson

A talented fellow named Jack
Has often been wasted on smack
But as movie stars go
He's a consummate pro
So we're happy to cut him some slack

In school he was voted Class Clown
Gaining serious local renown
As a quick witted guy
With a glint in his eye
Who was meant to be Hollywood bound

Jack moved west to L.A. with a goal
To beg and beseech and cajole
His way in to parts
In the cinema arts
With the passion he had in his soul

In second rate films he was cast
And although he was having a blast
He was stuck in a rut
With his head up his butt
And ambitions that seemed to be dashed

But then with the part of George Hanson
He arrived, like the late David Janssen
Easy Rider's the flick
Where he shouted 'nick nick'
When a young Peter Fonda was handsome

Then in Five Easy Pieces he starred
As a man psychologically scarred
For his brilliant rendition
He gained recognition
And note of the highest regard

Later Roman Polanski induced
Jack to act in a film he produced
As a glib private eye
With big fishes to fry
Who pursued a young gal who'd vamoosed

In The Shining he scared us to bits
As a man who lost touch with his wits
And embarked on a tear
In the cool mountain air
When his sanity went on the fritz

Harry Nilsson

Harry Nilsson was gifted and strange
And displayed a remarkable range
In his splendid career
Spanning many a beer
In the songs that he wrote and arranged

He was born in New York one fine day
Then his family moved west to L.A.
Where he grew to a man
And his music began
To get published for radio play

He sold three of his songs to Phil Spector
Who was known as a talent detector
Then he joined RCA
And began making hay
In the finicky show business sector

The Beatles liked Harry a lot
Soon millions of records were bought
He was much in demand
Earning hundreds of grand
But he often was sad and distraught

Nilsson Schmilsson was maybe the best
Of the records his studio pressed
But he always preferred
Songs that rarely were heard
While eschewing commercial success

Now it's been many years since he died
With his wife and six kids by his side
But his music survives
For the joy it derives
From a rocky but wonderful ride

Richard Nixon

A fellow they called Tricky Dick
By and large wasn't stupid or thick
But in '72
In a cranial coup
He lost touch with his brain really quick

He was seeking to get re-elected
And a landslide was fully expected
His opponent was weak
And a bit of a geek
With a running mate no one respected

Then the Watergate break-in took place
And a nation would soon have to brace
For a turbulent ride
Where the President lied
Causing singular angst and disgrace

Two reporters named Carl and Bob
Believed that the caper was odd
So they followed some leads
Finding many misdeeds
And they did a remarkable job

That election in '72
Resulted in term number two
For Dick and his aides
Who were dodging grenades
As distrust and malevolence grew

The Watergate thing wouldn't die
Bob and Carl continued to pry
They were clearly obsessed
And they never digressed
Spiro Agnew was caught in a lie

Nixon's minions did other bad acts
In a scheme that was riddled with cracks
Then the shit hit the fan
When the cover-up plan
Was exposed and they all got the axe

Many aides were both tried and convicted
And Nixon himself was depicted
As out of control
With an odious soul
That was often confused and conflicted

With impeachment proceedings in store
Nixon couldn't endure any more
Of the shame and the stress
Of the Watergate mess
And announced he would govern no more

But many believed and still do
That behaviour like this wasn't new
Or unique to one man
With a dastardly plan
But insisted he hadn't a clue

Chuck Norris

A fellow we know as Chuck Norris
Makes movies that usually bore us
Where predictable themes
Flow like particle beams
With plots formulaic and porous

He was born in a Midwestern State
With a bit of red hair on his pate
Where the Sooners play ball
Every Winter and Fall
And they always have beef on their plate

Chuck enjoyed martial arts for a time
As he thought it was cool and sublime
Then the acting bug bit
So he opted to split
To make movies while still in his prime

The films that he's made are forgettable
With plot lines banal and untenable
But they made him as rich
As a son of a bitch
That he made them at all is regrettable

Chuck believes in the literal word
Of The Bible, where wrath was incurred
When sins were committed
Which wasn't permitted
And punishment then was conferred

He believes owning guns is his right
Though they fill many people with fright
And with bullets as well
From the rifle cartel
Whose net profits are high as a kite

Chuck doesn't want gays getting wed
The idea consumes him with dread
He voted for Mitt
Thinks Obama's a twit
And deserves a swift kick in the head

He's the subject of hundreds of jokes
Told by numerous ladies and blokes
There are websites created
Where gags are related
By various fun loving folks

Barack Obama

A fellow we know as Barack
Is more of a dove than a hawk
He's a liberal at heart
And demonstrably smart
Much like Johann Sebastian Bach

In Hawaii he says he was born
Where the natives are wont to adorn
Many tourists with leis
When they land for their stays
Where the weather's consistently warm

But some think that Mr. Obama
Arrived through the slit of his Momma
In an African land
Mostly covered in sand
And it's caused much annoyance and drama

At Harvard he studied the law
Where the winters are windy and raw
Then he dated Michelle
And she caused him to swell
When he saw what was under her bra

As a law school professor he taught
For minority justice he fought
For State Senate he ran
With great verve and elan
But a much higher office he sought

With his wit and his great erudition
He soon would be in a position
To run for the job
That was held by a knob
Known as Bush, who was frequently fishin'

For the ticket he ran against Hillary
Whose husband was easy to pillory
For being so randy
With anyone handy
Who'd service his hardened artillery

Barack out-campaigned her and won
Much support for his ultimate run
Against Johnny McCain
And a gal with no brain
With a butt that was second to none

He selected a fellow named Joe
A seasoned political pro
To run as his mate
He had plugs on his pate
Where his hair was refusing to grow

Then a race for the White House ensued
Where a grumpy old man and a dude
Debated and smeared
In their ads that appeared
While Ms. Palin made trousers protrude

Barack won the general election
And lots of unbridled affection
But with promises broke
He turned in to a joke
With a spying and drone predilection

Conan O'Brien

A fellow called Conan O'Brien
Has plenty of fish to be fryin'
Many laughs he incites
He produces and writes
But he's never had sex with Meg Ryan

Near Boston this fellow arrived
As a baby his parents contrived
His surroundings were plush
Mom and Dad were both flush
Growing up he was never deprived

At Harvard he ran the Lampoon
Which has published for many a moon
Making good-natured fun
With the stories they run
Which the students eat up with a spoon

After college he joined SNL
And his bank account started to swell
For The Simpsons he wrote
He was quick with a joke
Like Rob Petrie and Buddy Sorrell

In two thousand and nine he replaced
Jay Leno, and soon he was based
In the town of L.A.
Where the Rams used to play
And a strange way of life is embraced

But Leno would soon change his mind
About leaving his program behind
A fiasco ensued
Conan felt he got screwed
As his ratings and spirit declined

The network asked Conan to switch
His time slot to settle this glitch
But he didn't agree
So he told NBC
That he wouldn't perform as their bitch

One year later he told them good-bye
With nary a tear in his eye
Then he joined TBS
For a pile of largesse
Which will last 'til his grandchildren die

Carroll O'Connor

An actor named Carroll O'Connor
Is a man we continue to honor
With posthumous praise
For his thespian days
Before he succumbed as a goner

He was born long ago in Manhattan
Not far from the island of Staten
His Dad practiced law
And his Mom wore a bra
As they dined on potatoes au gratin

Carroll acted when going to school
In Dublin, where leprechauns rule
Then in Europe he stayed
To develop his trade
As his wife took good care of his tool

In the fifties he crosses the ocean
And returns to the States with a notion
Of plying his craft
Like Glenn Ford and George Raft
Who were great at portraying emotion

Carroll landed small parts for a spell
In movies that did fairly well
Soon his face became known
From the seeds he had sown
And his bank account started to swell

And then came the role of his life
In a comedy peppered with strife
Where a bigoted man
Tried to cope with his clan
Which included his dim-witted wife

For eight seasons he played Archie Bunker
In a show that was never a clunker
Where his daughter's young hubby
Got many a chubby
With which he was happy to plunk her

Archie wasn't a fan of minorities
Or orgies at frats and sororities
He was very right wing
In his castle a king
With cigars on his list of priorities

After All in the Family was done
Archie's Place had a pretty good run
But things weren't the same
Many thought it was lame
Unlike Maude, which had also been spun

But then 'In the Heat of the Night'
Came along, to O'Connor's delight
And for seven good years
Like Ted Danson in Cheers
He was blessed with a staff that could write

Carroll filled us with wonder and mirth
In the time he was here on this Earth
He stoll millions of hearts
He had talent and smarts
And he milked it for all it was worth

Yoko Ono

A lady we call Yoko Ono
Is still breathing, unlike Sonny Bono
She was married to John
Who is now dead and gone
And whose records we played on the phono

She was born in Japan long ago
Where a lot of rice paddies they grow
And there's plenty of quakes
And tsunamis with wakes
Also Geishas, who put on a show

Yoko's family had plenty of dough
In the forties, so off they would go
To the U.S. of A.
To escape from the fray
That was known as the Second World Woe

She met John and he split with his spouse
He liked what was under her blouse
And her panties as well
Yoko caused him to swell
So he bought her a car and a house

Together they wrote many songs
And they smoked marijuana in bongs
They had lust in their pants
They said 'give peace a chance'
Yoko often wore earth tone sarongs

John Lennon was killed by a clown
Who was looking for fame and renown
He and Yoko were walking
Mark Chapman was stalking
And then from behind shot him down

Yoko needed a calmness infusion
So she chose to go in to seclusion
Her life had been wrecked
In most every respect
In a moment of mental delusion

She returned to resume her career
And the causes she holds very dear
Now she's back in the arts
With her passion and smarts
But in public she's loath to appear

Roy Orbison

There once was a man known as Roy
Who was meek and withdrawn as a boy
But he won all our hearts
With his songs on the charts
That engendered both sadness and joy

He was born in the city of Vernon
In Texas, where drillers are yearnin'
To find lots of oil
Deep down in the soil
And Sundays converge for a sermon

Roy also resided in Wink
A town you can miss if you blink
Where football's adored
Roy was totally bored
And it pretty near drove him to drink

After high school he hadn't a plan
For transition from boy to a man
So he started to sing
In the era of swing
And the formative days of The Klan

But he wasn't a handsome young dude
With an image of sex to exude
So less talented jerks
Got the money and perks
And had sex with the women they wooed

Roy studied at North Texas State
Where the handsome Pat Boone was his mate
Pat was making good dough
And he later turned pro
When he still had real hair on his pate

Roy was singing part-time in a band
In a town that he barely could stand
He performed many gigs
Where the men from the rigs
Guzzled beer from a bottle or can

Then in Dallas he met Johnny Cash
At a radio fund raising bash
He was friendly and nice
And he offered advice
Then they had a few beers and some hash

To Sun Records is where Johnny said
He should go, so that's where he would head
When Sam Phillips heard Roy
He was gushing with joy
And a contract was soon put to bed

Roy's last concert 'A Black and White Night'
Was truly a magical sight
Where Roy and his peers
In a room serving beers
All took turns stepping up to the mike

In his work, spanning thirty-five years
Through a gamut of blood, sweat and tears
Roy enthralled and amazed
On the trail that he blazed
Which was better than working at Sears

Peter O'Toole

An actor named Peter O'Toole
Spent much of his time on a stool
Sipping gin in a bar
With a Cuban cigar
Looking totally dashing and cool

In the city of Leeds he was born
Where drinking warm beer is the norm
At a very young age
He was drawn to the stage
With a passionate urge to perform

Long before he was in his first flick
Peter acted at Bristol Old Vic
Doing Shakespeare and such
He was praised very much
Of the pack he was clearly the pick

He performed on the stage for 8 years
As he guzzled much whiskey and beers
And he then caught the eye
Of a Hollywood guy
In the land of Ford Motors and Sears

To Arabia Peter would go
To earn some American dough
As Lawrence he shined
Where much crude is refined
And a gal with no veil is a 'ho

Now the floodgates were open for Peter
And his offers got sweeter and sweeter
He got rich and well-known
And increasingly prone
To imbibing on booze by the litre

In 'My Favorite Year' he was splendid
And many an elbow he bended
In his role as a sot
Downing hooch by the shot
For an Oscar award he contended

'The Stunt Man' was stylish and weird
In the roundabout course that it steered
Peter shone once again
He was rated a '10'
As the critics and audience cheered

In a movie called 'Troy' Peter played
A guy far too old to get laid
Whose sons went to war
For the sake of a whore
Who was loaded with diamonds and jade

Now Peter O'Toole has expired
Having done all the things he desired
In his time on this Earth
He regaled us with mirth
And will always be loved and admired

Al Pacino

A fellow we know as Pacino
Is Italian, like Carlo Gambino
And a Hollywood star
Who is known near and far
Like Penelope Cruz, a Latino

He was born in The Empire State
In East Harlem, where life wasn't great
There were gangsters galore
Dumping bodies offshore
With cement for increasing their weight

Al quit school to pursue a career
On the stage where he longed to appear
In productions of plays
Where he hungered for praise
Which he got when he made his premiere

On Broadway he did very well
And his bank account started to swell
So he went to L.A.
Where he lives to this day
As a part of the movie cartel

But at first, on the coast there was stress
And not a whole lot of success
As he played minor parts
He was wasting his smarts
But he stuck to his guns nonetheless

Then Francis Ford Coppola phoned
From the opulent house that he owned
He wanted Pacino
To play the bambino
Of mafia boss Corleone

In The Godfather Al made a splash
For 35 thousand in cash
That is all he was paid
For the part he portrayed
Though the film was a box office smash

In Godfather II he repeated
His role and his efforts were greeted
With glowing reviews
All the press were enthused
With the way his persona was treated

Al was suddenly cream of the crop
And was loving his view from the top
In Glengarry Glen Ross
He detested his boss
And in Serpico starred as a cop

In Scarface he played a real prick
With a load that was short by a brick
In Justice For All
All his fans had a ball
With his darkly satirical schtick

It's too bad he made Godfather III
It's a movie that's painful to see
But he couldn't say no
To the shitload of dough
Anted up by the powers that be

Sarah Palin

A gal from Alaska named Sarah
Arrived in the Tea Party era
Once she ran for VP
In the land of the free
And the home of the great Yogi Berra

In Idaho Sarah was born
Where they grow much potato and corn
She moved north as a child
Where the weather's not mild
And where down-filled pajamas are worn

She was truly a good looking broad
By the time she got wedded to Todd
In Wasila they dwelled
As a couple they jelled
As they pledged their devotion to God

Sarah soon was the Mayor of the town
And a lady of local renown
She and Todd had some kids
They ate moose meat and squids
And were happy as Bozo the Clown

Then Sarah got gubernatorial
And her manner of dress more sartorial
As the boss of her State
She had lots on her plate
And was was featured in many pictorial

Then a national gig came along
John McCain needed somebody strong
He picked Sarah to be
His potential VP
As he liked how she looked in a thong

Sarah scored as a media hit
But she soon would be known as a twit
With a modest IQ
Who had nary a clue
And a shortage of tools in her kit

The ticket of Sarah and John
Didn't rivet the public for long
They got beat by Barack
Who could preach to the flock
Johnny's judgment was proved to be wrong

With a luckless campaign now behind her
The Tea Party wined her and dined her
She had time on her hands
And fit in to their plans
So they took her aside and refined her

Sarah's still cashing in on her fame
And the fact people still know her name
She does books and TV
She does nothing for free
She's becoming one very rich dame

Walter Payton

On the field they described him as 'Sweetness'
In his legs he was loaded with fleetness
When he carried the ball
Many records would fall
As he rose to unrivaled eliteness

He was born in southeast Mississippi
Where the air very seldom is nippy
Where Old Glory is flown
And where peanuts are grown
Then are processed and made in to Skippy

He played football at Jefferson High
Where his talent and strength caught the eye
Of scouts and recruiters
Who soon were his suitors
And offered him gifts on the sly

Jackson State was the school he attended
Where Robert Brazile was befriended
Where there weren't many fights
As there weren't any whites
So no turf to be breached or defended

In a game back in 72
He became part of football's who's who
Scoring seven TDs
With comparative ease
Then the team went and hoisted a few

After college he went to the Bears
As the answer to all of their prayers
Their offence had sunk
To the point where it stunk
So a high draft selection was theirs

Then for 12 quite remarkable years
Payton turned a whole league on its ears
Earning plenty of loot
For the way he could scoot
Which was better then working at Sears

At age 33 he retired
With his wife and the dough they'd acquired
But a liver disease
Brought old Walt to his knees
And at age 45 he expired

Joe Pesci

A talented fellow named Joe
Has earned himself plenty of dough
Playing hoodlums and thugs
Filling people with slugs
Any time that it seemed apropos

Joe Pesci was born in New York
Where the Yankees compete in a sport
Every Summer and Fall
With a glove and a ball
And a bat sometimes loaded with cork

As a barber Joe worked for a spell
Cutting hair and anointing with jell
He'd performed on the stage
At an earlier age
But it didn't go terribly well

Then at age 36 he was hired
For a film that is widely admired
Raging Bull brought him fame
And artistic acclaim
Which he'd quietly always desired

After that Joe was cast quite a lot
In films that more often than not
Were considered mundane
Unlike Citizen Kane
They premiered and were quickly forgot

But in Goodfellas Pesci broke through
As a guy who was part of a crew
Stealing cargo and cash
And the film was a smash
From the day that it made its debut

Home Alone was a box office hit
Where Joe played a blundering twit
Who attempted a theft
When a youngster was left
By himself to get by on his wit

When he played Cousin Vinny he killed
The producers were totally thrilled
Many tickets were sold
Joe was box office gold
As the star of the film he was billed

But Casino was likely the best
Of the movies with which he was blessed
To be given the role
Of a man with no soul
Who was often placed under arrest

In the film he played Nicky Santoro
Who inflicted much violence and sorrow
As a matter of course
With no hint of remorse
'Til his friends whacked him in to tomorrow

He is semi-retired these days
And involved in the staging of plays
He's got plenty of loot
He's a wealthy old coot
And the master of all he surveys

Michelle 'Mama' Phillips

In the 60's a chick named Michelle
Caused manhoods to stiffen and swell
With her sensuous pout
Many chubbies she'd sprout
Long before people talked on a cell

She was born in Long Beach, near L.A.
Where the surfers ride waves every day
As they try not to drown
And the sun makes them brown
So they all look like Cassius Clay

With the Mamas and Papas she sang
Where great lyrics and melodies sprang
Their arrangements were smart
But it all fell apart
When she humped Denny Doherty's wang

Michelle learned to sing as a teen
To join up with a band she was keen
And to travel the Earth
Spreading music and mirth
Earning fame and a truckload of green

Papa John was her hubby and boss
Who did drugs and imbibed in the sauce
He was musically great
But too young met his fate
Like Dan Blocker, who charmed us as Hoss

'Papa' John Phillips

A fellow they called Papa John
Smoked more grass than he had on his lawn
His music was magic
His habits were tragic
He died all dishevelled and wan

In Virginia John Phillips was reared
Where tobacco is ripened and sheared
His old man was a sot
Who got wasted a lot
So his vision quite often was bleared

After high school John wandered a bit
He tried college, but soon he would quit
Then the folk singing fad
Got a hold of this lad
So away to New York he would flit

With The Journeymen John got a gig
And he hoped to be making it big
In the earliest days
Of the folk singing craze
Making music young people could dig

Later on he met Denny and Cass
Quite a talented laddie and lass
Then Michelle came along
And inflated his dong
With her face and her cute little ass

Soon the Mamas and Papas arrived
With the singular sound they contrived
Scoring numerous hits
We all loved them to bits
Now there's only one left who's survived

They played concerts that always sold out
Like The Beatles, who sang Twist and Shout
But after three years
Just like Brittney Spears
Many problems were starting to sprout

John split up with the group and his wife
In a flurry of rancour and strife
Then he set out alone
With a mind to atone
For the way he'd been living his life

But he had many demons inside him
And many a source to provide him
With smack and cocaine
Which infested his brain
When there wasn't a compass to guide him

John passed on after 65 years
Of great triumphs and thousands of tears
He was cursed, he was blessed
And failed many a test
But was music to all of our ears

Brad Pitt

Brad Pitt's proved his worth at his trade
In the excellent movies he's made
In Snatch he was splendid
And roundly commended
A gypsy named Mick he portrayed

Gwyneth Paltrow and Brad used to date
Quite often she made him inflate
She looked good in a thong
But it didn't last long
He was seeking a permanent mate

Brad met Jennifer Aniston later
And quickly decided to date her
They were married a while
They were living in style
He probed down below her equator

But Jennifer bored him to bits
Their marriage was clearly the pits
So he gave her the boot
And one half of his loot
And their condo in sunny St. Kitts

But before he showed Jenny the door
He already was mopping the floor
With a gal name Jolie
Who was foorloose and free
And made his testosterone soar

On her lips you could park a small car
They're as fat as a Cuban cigar
They were surgically puffed
And symmetrically stuffed
On her butt there's a permanent scar

Valerie Plame

A lady named Valerie Plame
Was considered by some as 'fair game'
She was sold up the creek
With a dastardly leak
To one goofy ex-President's shame

She worked as a CIA spy
And routinely made deals on the sly
With much valor and stealth
At great risk to her health
If she ever was caught in a lie

Her hubby's a fellow named Joe
A politically consummate pro
With connections galore
Both at home and offshore
He has always been much in the know

Bush and Cheney were keen to attack
The faraway land of Iraq
But they needed support
So they cooked a report
Then proceeded to pillage and sack

They based their invasion decision
In spite of much global division
On a sinister lie
Half a million would die
From a case of acute tunnel vision

But then Joe wrote a piece for the press
Causing Cheney and Bushy distress
He exposed their deception
And raised our perception
And then came the Valerie mess

The White House exposed her vocation
Which resulted in traumatization
For Val and her clan
Just to punish her man
For exposing their misinformation

Scooter Libby took all of the blame
In the matter of Valerie Plame
When he fell on his sword
For a jerk he adored
And George W. Bush was his name

Cole Porter

There once was a man known as Cole
Who is now six feet deep in a hole
He's been gone 50 years
But his work still endears
Like a leisurely neighborhood stroll

He was born in the Hoosier State
Where he rarely went out on a date
His family had loot
And much privilege to boot
Both his parents believed he was straight

At age 6 he could play violin
When he wedged it just under his chin
Then piano he learned
To write music he yearned
But that wasn't the wish of his kin

After high school he studied at Yale
Where his friends he would often regale
With the songs he'd composed
When the bar rooms had closed
Or they'd run out of co-eds to nail

Cole himself was demonstrably gay
Which was very taboo in his day
As a matter of trust
It was never discussed
But the rumors did not go away

He wrote 300 songs while at school
Causing Broadway producers to drool
For a talent and flair
They regarded as rare
Gay or straight, he was gifted and cool

After Yale he resided in France
Where he honed his unique song and dance
But his confidence fell
When his work didn't sell
And it hurt like a kick in the pants

To New York he decided to go
Where he authored a musical show
That was nicely received
He was jazzed and relieved
And his bank account started to grow

He wrote 20 more plays, mostly hits
As the orchestras played in the pits
He was great in his time
With his rhythm and rhyme
In the city of glamour and glitz

Elvis Presley

He arrived in northeast Mississippi
Where moonshine is drank when it's nippy
And where gospel is sung
As the church bells are rung
And the dew on magnolias is drippy

Elvis Presley would answer his calling
With the charm of his smile and his drawling
Both his presence and voice
Made promoters rejoice
Though some thought his gyrations appalling

His recording debut 'That's All Right'
Turned him in to a star overnight
In July '54
With his foot in the door
His career was about to take flight

With fame he was suddenly rife
Then the army came in to his life
He completed his hitch
Putting off getting rich
Then he made Miss Priscilla his wife

Later on several movies he made
And for that he was handsomely paid
Though each picture was crap
With less substance than pap
Happy endings were always conveyed

But with all of the money and fame
There also was anguish and pain
His wife hit the road
He was hurt and it showed
His depression was hard to contain

In October of seventy-three
There was issued a final decree
Of divorce from Priscilla
Who moved to a villa
Along with their Lisa Marie

As Elvis continued his aging
His hormones would cease to be raging
Through the years many pills
For his various ills
Would assist in the shows he was staging

In his life he was gifted and kind
Then one day both his body and mind
Faded out of our sight
Like a dream in the night
As he left all his troubles behind

Lisa Marie Presley

A lady named Lisa Marie
Long ago sat on Elvis's knee
As a pudgy young lass
Full of colic and gas
Wearing diapers to soak up her pee

Her Mom is a gal called Priscilla
Who has coats made of mink and chinchilla
She was in Naked Gun
Which was silly and fun
Now she's saggy and over the hill-a

Now Lisa Marie's fully grown
And some seeds of her own she has sown
She's had four different hubbies
And most sported chubbies
She's never been killed by a drone

Michael Jackson was one of her men
He came close to a stretch in the pen
For sleeping with lads
And exposing his 'nads
While they listened to Beat It and Ben

Later Nicolas Cage came along
And he liked how she looked in a thong
So they quickly got wed
And got naked in bed
Three months later she colored him 'gone'

Now she's hitched to her music director
Who isn't a jerk, like Phil Spector
Michael Lockwood's her man
He's her number one fan
And well known in the show business sector

This lady called Lisa Marie
Now lives in a land 'cross the sea
On a London estate
Near Prince William and Kate
Where the locals drink Guinness and tea

Victoria Principal

Victoria Principal played
A lady who often got laid
By Bobby, her mate
When she made him inflate
Like his former main squeeze, Jenna Wade

She was born in the land of Japan
Where a woman must bow to her man
And where wrestlers are fat
When they go to the mat
And where veggies get fried in a pan

As a youngster she studied ballet
And modeled for nominal pay
But to act was her aim
For the fortune and fame
So at twenty she moved to L.A.

Victoria struggled a lot
On the coast, even though she was hot
With a gleam in her eye
But her dream wouldn't die
In the city where movies are shot

In a Paul Newman flick she impressed
And she won an award as the best
Of the newcomer crop
Though the film was a flop
As her journey to stardom progressed

Then in Earthquake she landed a part
As a gal who resembled a tart
Who looked good in tight jeans
And who stole many scenes
In a movie more goofy than smart

But then came the role of her life
Where she played the long suffering wife
Of a stylish young dude
In the business of crude
Overwrought by perpetual strife

In Dallas Victoria shone
And millions of laddies were drawn
To her fabulous knockers
Which bloated their Dockers
And made them run off to the john

Now Victoria's semi-retired
And by millions beloved and admired
For her charity deeds
Helping people with needs
With the cash and the clout she's acquired

Gerry Rafferty

There once was a fellow named Gerry
Who grew up with the songs of Chuck Berry
Then wrote songs of his own
And got very well known
For imbibing, but not being merry

In Scotland young Gerry arrived
Where a lot of great booze is contrived
And slowly refined
So when people unwind
They will never be whiskey-deprived

His old man was a terrible sot
Who started most days with a shot
And most evenings as well
In the local hotel
Or at home with a bottle he'd bought

Gerry's mother was hoping her lad
Wouldn't follow the path of his Dad
So she taught him to sing
For the joy it could bring
Through the natural talent he had

With The Humblebums Gerry debuted
As a bright 22-year old dude
In a folk singing band
And they traveled the land
Playing tunes as the locals got stewed

Then a record producer was drawn
To his voice, and he soon signed him on
To make an LP
For a nominal fee
But the disc was a bit of a yawn

Later Gerry would found Stealers Wheel
And the band had some instant appeal
With a number one song
But they didn't last long
As they couldn't agree on a deal

He went solo and did very well
Many millions of records he'd sell
But his personal life
Was abundant with strife
As he struggled with demons from hell

On an album called City to City
We heard how amazingly pretty
Words and music could be
To the utmost degree
When created by someone so witty

But fortune and fame he eschewed
As it made him upset and unglued
He was blessed but tormented
And rarely contented
But brilliant when in the right mood

For a year he went in to seclusion
Which caused much concern and confusion
There were rumors abound
That his health wasn't sound
And he suffered from mental delusion

Gerry Rafferty died one sad day
When his mind and his body gave way
But his music remains
In our hearts and our brains
Where he'll always have somewhere to play

Harold Ramis

There once was a fellow named Ramis
Who became very wealthy and famous
In the time he was here
With his whimsy and cheer
And his wonderful sense of insaneness

Harold Ramis was born in Chicago
Where Elliot Ness showed bravado
When fighting the mob
Was his primary job
And Capone was the main desperado

Harold started his path to success
In the business of humor and jest
In the newspaper game
Earning local acclaim
Quite a talent for words he possessed

Second City provided the stage
For his comedy coming of age
Where he flaunted his smarts
In the theater arts
For no more than the minimum wage

After that he was off to L.A.
And New York for the glamor and pay
Of film and TV
Where he earned his degree
And began making serious hay

He wrote and he acted in Stripes
Which made fun of the stereotypes
Of the business of war
It made money galore
On TV it still charms and delights

With his writing he prospered and thrived
From the humorous scripts he contrived
Bringing wonder and mirth
To the people of Earth
Now he's sadly no longer alive

So we say 'Rest in Peace' to a man
Who put many great films in the can
Now he's gone, not forgot
And at rest in his plot
He was clearly no flash in the pan

Ronald Reagan

As an actor he wasn't the best
But he knew how to feather his nest
And be nicely connected
To get him elected
With humor and charm he was blessed

As governor Reagan would serve
California with gusto and verve
He was far to the right
And his future was bright
With contributed cash in reserve

To be President Reagan aspired
So advisers and mentors were hired
To assist in his quest
At his whim and behest
To procure the support he required

He lost in two federal elections
But gained many voters' affections
Then in run number three
Filled his party with glee
As the nation was changing directions

In The White House he served for 8 years
Through a gamut of blood, sweat and tears
He survived getting shot
Took vacations a lot
But was loved by his minions and peers

Then the Contra affair reared its head
Where Reagan was spending some bread
He illegally raised
Then appeared to be dazed
Back when Oliver North was a fed

By the end of his time in D.C.
He rarely appeared on TV
He took numerous naps
And had many a lapse
Like a punch drunk Muhammad Ali

Reagan died in two thousand and four
And was flooded with kudos galore
For his redefinition
Of Beltway tradition
Like no one accomplished before

Harry Reasoner

There once was a fellow named Harry
Who was born on the Iowa prairie
Where corn grown on cobs
Renders thousands of jobs
And tornadoes are totally scary

Minnesota is where he was schooled
Where Jesse Ventura once ruled
Harry's primary aim
Was the media game
For the challenge and passion it fueled

After fighting the Germans and Japs
With millions of other young chaps
Harry joined CBS
On his road to success
Where his talents were used to the max

In the earliest days of TV
He worked for the powers that be
Doing news and narration
Was Harry's vocation
He suited his job to a T

60 Minutes is where he became
A man of substantial acclaim
For 2 years he was there
In prime time on the air
Where reporters were given free rein

ABC later lured him away
When they offered him copious pay
To deliver the news
Harry couldn't refuse
Eight years later he'd worn out his stay

Then from '78 'til he passed
Many noted awards he amassed
60 Minutes once more
Brought him kudos galore
For the hard-hitting questions he asked

Harry's talent, by all estimations
Was bounded by no limitations
He worked hard at his job
Many hours he logged
But he always found time for libations

Burt Reynolds

A talented actor named Burt
Is known as a scamp and a flirt
And a man of great wit
Like John Cleese, who's a Brit
Pretty soon he'll be older than dirt

In Georgia Burt Reynolds was born
Where many were sad and forlorn
Many decades before
When the South lost the war
And had many dead soldiers to mourn

He played football at Florida State
Many scouts said his future was great
But he injured his knee
To a nasty degree
Then had trouble supporting his weight

When he couldn't compete in his sport
Burt left college and moved to New York
Where he went to auditions
For Broadway renditions
But most of his efforts fell short

He persisted in chasing his dream
On the finicky show business scene
And he landed some parts
In the theater arts
And the Harry S. Truman regime

With TV in it's earliest stage
That's when Burt had his coming of age
He moved west to L.A.
And got work right away
For much more than the minimum wage

After paying his dues on TV
Where he filled his producers with glee
Burt was primed for success
And a fancy address
And commanded a six-figure fee

Soon the world knew his face and his name
As his acting drew lavish acclaim
Many scripts came his way
And he bought a toupee
As he relished his fortune and fame

In Deliverance Burt got the part
Of a man with no song in his heart
In the film Semi-tough
He was keen for the muff
Of Jill Clayburgh, a pretty young tart

Starting Over gave Reynolds a chance
To deal with a broken romance
In a film called The End
Dom DeLuise, as his friend
Made us laugh 'til we peed in our pants

In Boogie Nights Burt was first-rate
As a guy who made manhoods inflate
With his x-rated flicks
Where promiscuous chicks
Had no trouble in getting a date

There is an old geezer named Burt
Who continues to thrill and divert
With his humor and skill
Though he's over the hill
Like that fatty who played Captain Kirk

Andy Rooney

There once was a man known as Rooney
Who was known as a bit of al loony
Full of wonder and mirth
In his time on this Earth
Now he's gone, just like Rosemary Clooney

He arrived back in 1919
Back when movies were wholesome and clean
In the Empire State
Where the Yankees were great
And all white, much unlike Ben Vereen

In the 40's he fought in the war
Where soldiers were killed by the score
At the end of that mess
Andy joined CBS
Where he'd have a great future in store

First he wrote a variety show
And its audience started to grow
It became a big hit
Partly due to his wit
Then big revenues started to flow

But it wasn't 'til '78
When gray hair was all over his pate
That he'd start making hay
In his singular way
When he'd skewer, deride and berate

Sixty Minutes was good long before
Andy Rooney walked in through their door
But his 5 minute bit
Was an overnight hit
And it prompted the ratings to soar

There were times when his comments offended
And he once was reproached and suspended
When in speaking his mind
He got in to a bind
But hard feelings were never intended

Andy worked 'til his 93rd year
And continued to charm and endear
'Til he quietly died
With his kids by his side
As his millions of fans shed a tear

Mickey Rooney

Mickey Rooney is now far away
From his opulent home in L.A.
After 93 years
Of blood, sweat and tears
He decided he'd worn out his stay

He was born in the Empire State
And always had much on his plate
Both on film and TV
He filled millions with glee
And was never hard up for a date

He was just 17 when he played
A young fellow who never got laid
By his co-starring chicks
In a series of flicks
That a Hollywood studio made

The first was 'A Family Affair'
Where Mickey could showcase his flair
Stealing many a scene
As an amorous teen
Full of angst and comedic despair

Andy Hardy he played with panache
Showing copious spirit and dash
Drawing glowing reviews
For the talent he oozed
In exchange for some serious cash

Judy Garland and Mickey were tight
As a team they could charm and delight
She could sing any tune
But expired too soon
And was often as high as a kite

In National Velvet he shone
With Liz Taylor, who also was strong
Mickey's role was just right
For a man of his height
Drawing kudos from hither and yon

Mickey always found time for romance
With his smile he could charm and entrance
Many times he got wed
In the life that he led
He had many a bulge in his pants

Almost 200 movies he did
Starting out as a one-year old kid
In commercials and plays
Drawing copious praise
As his agent was flipping his lid

The world now has said 'au revoir'
To a totally consummate star
Who arrived on this Earth
Full of wonder and mirth
And has left it much better by far

Diana Ross

A lady we know as Diana
Had a hairdo the size of Montana
When she burst on the scene
At the age of nineteen
She was hot, just like Lola Falana

She was born in the Wolverine State
And made many a manhood inflate
Both at home and abroad
With her face and her bod
She was often asked out on a date

With two friends she began her career
On the musical course she would steer
Seeking fortune and fame
And artistic acclaim
When she still wore a training brassiere

The Supremes were a roaring success
All the girls had a fancy address
Ample revenues flowed
But ten years on the road
Caused professional angst and distress

So Diana set out on her own
And before very long she was known
For her talent and flare
And her long flowing hair
From L.A. to Sierra Leone

Mickey Rourke

An actor we call Mickey Rourke
Is a dude who was born in New York
Many roles he has played
In the movies he's made
In Barfly he made himself hork

His first major part was in Diner
In The Wrestler he sported a shiner
With Kim Basinger, Mickey
Had many a quickie
Involving her gorgeous vaginer

For a while Mickey worked as a fighter
Like Mike Tyson, the infamous biter
And he never got whipped
Many punches he slipped
But his future in acting was brighter

In Sin City he truly was great
In the character he would create
It was pure neo-noir
For his vast repertoire
And it did very well at the gate

Mickey's always been strangely unique
Never part of a Hollywood clique
Many risks he will take
Some would call him a flake
Certain others would call him a freak

His face has been surgically changed
From cosmetic procedures arranged
To repair all the flaws
On his eyes and his jaws
That were suffered when blows were exchanged

But through all of the good and the bad
And the various troubles he's had
Mickey always has thrived
In the roles he's contrived
As a hero or dastardly cad

Babe Ruth

A legend of baseball Babe Ruth
Was considered unkempt and uncouth
He was lazy and fat
But a whiz with a bat
From the time he played ball as a youth

He was born in the town of the Oriole
Where ball games were played at Memorial
Many hot dogs he ate
In the Chesapeake State
Where the forests were lush and arboreal

To reform school young George would be sent
When he'd clearly developed a bent
For committing bad deeds
As he sowed his wild seeds
In a youth that was clearly misspent

At St. Mary's Industrial School
Where the discipline bordered on cruel
Babe met Brother Matthias
Who made him more pious
And stopped him from acting the fool

That's when baseball got George's attention
And soon he began his ascension
To riches and fame
Just for playing a game
With much beer when he needed a quenchin'

He played in the minors at first
Where he wasn't too well reimbursed
Many innings he pitched
With a ball that was stitched
And with brewskies quenched many a thirst

To the majors Babe Ruth got promoted
Fenway Park is where fans are devoted
To cheering their teams
On their lush field of dreams
While on pizza and beer they get bloated

While the Babe was a star on the hill
Where his fastball resembled a pill
He moved to right field
For the bat he could wield
And to put much more cash in the till

But the Sox sold their star to the Yanks
Of New York, where there's plenty of skanks
Soon his talent took flight
He drank booze every night
And he downed many burgers and franks

In one year Babe hit 60 home runs
Long before George M. Steinbrenner's sons
Took the reins from their Dad
Who was stark raving mad
But had limitless sources of funds

At a very young age Babe was done
But he managed a wonderful run
Through much glory and strife
On the base path of life
He had many a day in the sun

Winona Ryder

A lady we know as Winona
Is known from L.A. to Daytona
On the silvery screen
Starting out as a teen
She's played many a quirky persona

In 'Lucas' she played her first role
Where her character tried to console
A nerdy young mate
Who could not get a date
With a cutie who captured his soul

Then in Beetlejuice Ryder impressed
In her role as a teenager dressed
In Gothic attire
With brimstone and fire
And darkness this gal was obsessed

In 'Great Balls of Fire' she played
A girl far too young to get laid
But she married her cuz
Who was labeled a scuzz
And a horny old man who had strayed

After that came unbridled success
Lots of cash and a fancy address
For this talented lass
With a marvelous ass
Who is loaded with skill and finesse

Carl Sagan

He looked up at the vastness of space
And how all the stars interlace
In a massive expanse
By design or by chance
And it put a big smile on his face

Carl Sagan was born in the State
Where the Rangers and Islanders skate
At a time of depression
And Nazi oppression
Inspired by malice and hate

As a child he was thoughtful and curious
Checking out both both the valid and spurious
While hoping to see
What the future might be
And whether or not it should worry us

He went to museums a lot
On his way to becoming self-taught
He asked questions galore
Then came back and asked more
With much wonder and joy he was fraught

Carl taught at Cornell while he wrote
More than 600 papers of note
And best sellers as well
Made his bank balance swell
He could always be good for a quote

He wrote Contact, which Hollywood took
From a clever, provocative book
To the silvery screen
Rated PG Thirteen
Moving faster than light was its hook

With Cosmos he changed how mankind
Observes how the stars are aligned
And how much isn't known
And what's carved in to stone
With the use of his wonderful mind

Sagan died in his 63rd year
On a day when we all shed a tear
But his spirit remains
In our souls and our brains
As he travels the final frontier

Colonel Harland Sanders

Kentucky Fried Chicken he founded
With growth that amazed and astounded
As his empire grew
Many chickens were slew
As his sales and his profits abounded

In the year 1930 he started
Cooking birds that were freshly departed
Back in Corbin, Kentucky
Much feathers he'd plucky
A road to success he had charted

He franchised his product and brand
All across every State in the land
And in Canada too
He had business to do
On a scale quite ambitiously grand

Near Toronto the Colonel located
When his mansion down south was vacated
Mississauga was home
'Cross the nation he'd roam
To ensure all his patrons were sated

Through the decades we have all have partook
In the goodies his outlets would cook
Many teeth we have picked
Many fingers we've licked
And our loyalty never was shook

The Colonel passed on in Kentucky
In his life he worked hard and got lucky
As did many around him
Success always found him
Down south and in land of canucky

Martin Scorcese

A fellow named Martin Scorcese
Is alive, much unlike Patrick Swayze
He's made movies galore
Often teeming with gore
Now he's old, but as fresh as a daisy

He was born in the Borough of Queens
Where he later would shoot many scenes
His folks were Sicilians
He's made many millions
From talent instilled in his genes

Early on he was keen to pursue
The Priesthood in order to do
What his parents preferred
In pursuit of The Word
He had piety up the wazoo

But a passion for movies took hold
So he followed a path that was bold
And fraught with distress
And much fiscal duress
But today he is box office gold

Mean Streets was his first major flick
And the critics all thought it was slick
As a dark slice of life
Where a gun or a knife
Could get rid of a Jew or a mick

But the best of his work was to come
His career was just starting to hum
Like Robert Di Nero
A great anti-hero
It seemed like he had a green thumb

Martin's movies are sometimes offbeat
And often eccentrically sweet
King of Comedy showed
How a brain could corrode
After Hours was truly a treat

In Goodfellas Martin conveyed
How a mobster could best be portrayed
Cape Fear made us cringe
When a man on the fringe
Carried out nasty plans he had made

But Casino stands out most of all
As a film that could shock and enthrall
With its pace and its plot
It will not be forgot
Like the hairline of Robert Duvall

Steven Seagal

A two-fisted fellow named Steven
Starts many a movie by grievin'
When family or friend
Meets a horrible end
Then he promptly sets out to get even

He was born in The Wolverine State
Down south from the Mackinaw Strait
In the city of Lansing
Where Motown's financing
Is still very much on their plate

Martial arts took up much of his time
Before he began fighting crime
On the silvery screen
As a killing machine
In an era of moral decline

Steven's movies have won no awards
But we still go to see them in hordes
Watching justice get served
And our freedoms preserved
In a way that excites and absorbs

Hard to Kill made the world know his name
As a man who somehow overcame
Seven years in a coma
And lost his persona
Then wanted to know who to blame

Out for Justice was eye-for-an-eye
Where Steven went after the guy
Who murdered his buddy
And left him all bloody
To shudder and whimper and die

Under Siege was especially lame
And devoid of artistic acclaim
It had numerous flaws
And they stuck in our craws
That he made it at all is a shame

But in spite of the hostile reviews
Steven always finds ways to bemuse
With the template approach
Of a basketball coach
As a way to delight and enthuse

Neil Sedaka

Neil Sedaka was born one fine day
In Brooklyn, New York, USA
He began singing tunes
As a teen in saloons
Where the patrons all thought he was gay

Later on, with his musical flair
He was heard many times on the air
He had numerous hits
Loved by youngsters with zits
And he soon was a rich millionaire

His girlfriend was once Carole King
Together they'd write and they'd sing
And have sex when aroused
But they never espoused
It was only a casual fling

Through the sixties and decades beyond
Many wonderful records he spawned
His cachet has endured
As his fans have matured
Like a registered government bond

Neil's music is whiter than rice
His CDs can be had for a price
He sings really high
Like a castrated guy
Or a dude with his 'nads in a vise

Bob Seger

Bob Seger was born in the State
Where the great Gordie Howe used to skate
And the Tigers play ball
Every Summer and Fall
And you're never too far from a lake

Ann Arbor is where he was reared
And embarked on the course that he steered
Reaching fortune and fame
And creative acclaim
Always sporting long hair and a beard

Little Richard gave Bob inspiration
For his sound and on-stage presentation
Elvis Presley as well
Singing Heartbreak Hotel
Helped to build his artistic foundation

With The Decibels Seger began
A music career that has spanned
More than 50 great years
Many whiskeys and beers
And more travel than most can withstand

With The Omens he later performed
Back when rock and roll music was scorned
By many old timers
In taverns and diners
The music was evil, they warned

Commercial success then arrived
When a rock and roll band was contrived
Called The Bob Seger System
When Motown dismissed 'im
And ever since then he has thrived

Later on Bob went solo, but found
He required a raunchier sound
So in '74
He was touring once more
With a band very skilled and renowned

Silver Bullet scored numerous hits
The radio loved them to bits
They got written about
Every concert sold out
When our faces were covered with zits

In Night Moves Bob sang of an urge
And the rapid testosterone surge
Of a horny young dude
Who was keen to get nude
When a chance to get lucky emerged

Live Bullet was maybe the best
Album like it that ever was pressed
Like a Rock was a smash
Earning shitloads of cash
Nine Tonight further feathered his nest

These days Seger is still doing shows
In the only vocation he knows
Many fans from his youth
Now are long in the tooth
And need help getting in to their clothes

Jerry Seinfeld

He was born in the Empire State
Where the Rangers and Islanders skate
In pursuit of a cup
As a Jew he grew up
Now he's built up a massive estate

Jerry started his stand-up career
And the course that he wanted to steer
In comedy bars
Where wannabe stars
Try to make people smile ear to ear

The Tonight Show booked Jerry to play
A five minute bit in L.A.
In the year '81
And he hit a home run
Ed and Johnny were both blown away

After that there were offers galore
And a wonderful future in store
For this wise cracking guy
With a glint in his eye
And a gift for comedic rapport

Near the end of the Reagan regime
Jerry followed a hunch and a dream
Of a show on TV
And approached NBC
To propose an unusual scheme

A show about nothing was pitched
And the network elites were bewitched
By its singular theme
It was never foreseen
Just how much they would all be enriched

Larry David, a colleague and chum
Was part of the show from day one
With his wonderful wit
Soon the show was a hit
Partly due to his comic green thumb

Seinfeld ran nine remarkable years
And boosted a lot of careers
All the cast in the show
Made a shitload of dough
Like the people who acted in Cheers

These days Jerry does stand-up and acts
But takes plenty of time to relax
With his Cuban cigars
And collection of cars
He's enjoying his life to the max

Peter Sellers

Peter Sellers was one of the best
With much talent and style he was blessed
He could play any role
From dramatic to droll
Though he often was dark and depressed

The Goon Show was Sellers' debut
As a part of Spike Milligan's crew
With their weirdness and wits
They did radio skits
And oodles of listeners they drew

In The Party the slapstick was wacky
With Sellers portraying a lackey
Though the critics weren't keen
He would own every scene
And it showcased his comical knacky

Dr. Strangelove propelled him to glory
He played multiple roles in the story
Of a nuclear scare
Full of angst and despair
With the President saying he's sorry

But when Sellers created Clouseau
Some hilarious magic would flow
With his wondrous depiction
Defying description
He'd steal every scene in the show

William Shatner

On Star Trek he played Captain Kirk
Who ventured where Romulans lurk
With his colleague McCoy
Who was in his employ
To treat people on board who got hurt

William Shatner was born in Quebec
The Province of René Levesque
And of Rocket Richard
Who could shoot really hard
But was often a pain in the neck

Shatner earned a degree from McGill
Then went west to develop his skill
On TV he was seen
Then the silvery screen
Long before there were Klingons to kill

On the stage he found work early on
Many theater goers were drawn
To this handsome young guy
With a glint in his eye
Many women were keen for his dong

But what brought him his fortune and fame
Which was always his primary aim
Was a low budget show
Where the ratings were low
Causing sponsors to whine and complain

In Star Trek he travelled through space
At warp speed, an astonishing pace
In the final frontier
Like a true pioneer
Representing his planet and race

Later on spinoff movies were made
For which he was handsomely paid
Star Trek IV was a smash
But the others were trash
As the novelty started to fade

But his acting career wasn't done
He was keen for more money and fun
So he played Denny Crane
Who was somewhat insane
From The Practice this series was spun

Boston Legal was brilliantly written
And millions of viewers were smitten
By Shatner's portrayal
Of an old alpha male
Whose dork very often would thicken

T.J. Hooker was also a show
That he starred in for oodles of dough
It lasted four years
In the era of Cheers
Where they guzzled fake shots of Old Crow

Shatner's hair and his waistline are gone
And his face is all puffy and wan
Now he sits by his pool
Taking dips to stay cool
While an immigrant's mowing his lawn

Charlie Sheen

An actor we call Charlie Sheen
Has traces of coke in his spleen
Many scenes he has made
Many roles he has played
On TV and the silvery screen

Platoon was his first major flick
And his work was regarded as slick
As a soldier in Nam
He would serve Uncle Sam
With a whole lot of commies to lick

But in Wall Street he really broke through
And his marketability grew
He was suddenly hot
Many offers he got
And he found many women to screw

He had married his sweetheart from school
But he had other plans for his tool
So he spread it around
Many babes were abound
Who would cause it to stiffen and drool

Charlie landed a role on Spin City
As a guy who was funny and flitty
The ratings were strong
Like the dope in his bong
And the scripts were refreshing and witty

But his next TV role was curtailed
When many a drug test he failed
Charlie often was faced
So they canned him post haste
When they thought he'd soon die or be jailed

Charlie lived with a couple of sluts
With nice facews and hooters and butts
Much narcotics were bought
He got ripped quite a lot
And each day went increasingly nuts

Now in various schemes he's involved
His arrangement at home was dissolved
He's a one-woman guy
Who enjoys getting high
So some issues are still unresolved

Cybill Shepherd

Cybill Shepherd is truly a treasure
By any acceptable measure
In her youth she was hot
When men humped her a lot
In their dreams, for vicarious pleasure

She was born in the Volunteer State
In the city where Elvis gained weight
And took too many pills
To diminish his ills
'Til he met with his ultimate fate

Cybill modeled a lot while in school
And was thought of as stylish and cool
With her beauty and body
Which wasn't too shoddy
She chubbified many a tool

Later Peter Bogdanovich saw
Cybill's face which had nary a flaw
So he gave her the part
Of a saucy young tart
He was jazzed by her je ne sais quoi

In The Last Picture Show Cybill played
A gal who was keen to get laid
In this movie production
With scenes of seduction
A splendid impression she made

Heartbreak Kid came along after that
Where Cybill portrayed a young brat
Who caused anguish and strife
For an innocent wife
Who was wed to a scum sucking rat

Cybill Shepherd made 46 more
Motion pictures at home and offshore
Some were good, others not
Some were lacking in plot
And wound up on the cutting room floor

Frank Sinatra

There once was a fellow named Frank
Who had plenty of cash in the bank
He was linked to the mob
Often traveled abroad
And got naked with many a skank

He began singing songs as a child
On the street, when the weather was mild
And in bars when it snowed
Where much alcohol flowed
All the locals were charmed and beguiled

Frank grew up as a handsome young dude
A lot of young ladies he wooed
In a club or a bar
Or back seat of a car
As Glenn Miller performed 'In The Mood'

He performed with 'The Hoboken Four'
Who sang 'til their tonsils were sore
Major Bowes saw their act
In a hall that was packed
With a crowd that was shouting for more

So the Major put Frank and the lads
Far away from their Moms and their Dads
Playing songs on the road
Where much talent they showed
And the groupies all ached for their 'nads

Frank then started his big band career
After catching the eye and the ear
Of the great Harry James
And some other big names
On the course he was destined to steer

Tommy Dorsey then wined him and dined him
To a personal contract he signed him
But after two years
Frank was keen to shift gears
So he put all that lifestyle behind him

As a soloist Frank made it big
As millions of fans came to dig
Both his dashing good looks
And his musical hooks
When they saw him performing a gig

He consorted with bad guys a lot
In Las Vegas, where battles were fought
By gun toting thugs
Over hookers and drugs
And a lot of poor buggers got shot

Many years ago Frank passed away
But we still hear his voice to this day
Through gladness and strife
He was bigger than life
And was rife with artistic cachet

Paul Sorvino

A talented guy named Sorvino
Like Mira, his actress bambino
Was born in New York
Where the Jets came up short
When their starting QB was Latino

He wrote copy for ads early on
But later he found himself drawn
To the Broadway domain
Fraught with glory and pain
Where he started as merely a pawn

In That Championship Season he showed
He was ready to carry the load
Of a star on the stage
For a lucrative wage
He was reaping the seeds he had sowed

After that there were offers galore
And a wonderful future in store
For this man on the rise
Of significant size
Playing roles both at home and offshore

In Goodfellas Paul played a boss
That his friend Henry Hill double crossed
And sent to the pen
With some other bad men
And did not pay the ultimate cost

He also played Sgt. Cerreta
A cop, like Bob Blake in Baretta
Law and Order was great
In the Empire State
Where there's many a nasty vendetta

Phil Spector

A genius-cum-wacko named Spector
Once excelled in the show business sector
As a maker of hits
Now in prison he sits
All alone, much like Hannibal Lecter

He was born long ago in New York
To a family who ate kosher pork
So that when he arrived
A Bris was contrived
Where they altered the end of his dork

In high school he played the guitar
With dreams of becoming a star
But there soon came a day
When he found his forté
In the lucrative role of a czar

In his heyday he shone like a star
Surpassing his rivals by far
His instinct was magic
His ending was tragic
When things got all weird and bizarre

Spector knew how to write and produce
But grew more and more strange and abstruse
Showing flashes of rage
As he reached middle age
Often faced on narcotics and juice

Lana Clarkson accompanied Phil
To his mansion one evening to swill
Some booze with the dude
And to maybe get screwed
By a guy who was mentally ill

Lana died from a shot to the brain
Which Phil tried his best to explain
As a wound self-inflicted
But many predicted
Acquittal could not be attained

Phil's trial did not go so well
And he's now serving time in a cell
With his awful toupee
And that's where he will stay
As a skinhead like Howie Mandel

Dusty Springfield

A hot looking gal known as Dusty
Caused lots of young men to get lusty
She had many great songs
And aroused many dongs
Even though she was not very busty

She was Mary O'Brien at birth
When she first set her feet on this Earth
Where the Queen is adored
And the French are deplored
And warm beer fills the punters with mirth

She was white, but had soul in her heart
She had many hit tunes on the chart
Like Wishin' and Hopin'
And songs about copin'
When everything's falling apart

In her time she could charm and endear
With a voice that we still like to hear
With her signature smile
She could charm and beguile
'Til she died in her 60th year

Bruce Springsteen

A rock & roll legend named Bruce
Has never been thick or obtuse
When it comes to his art
And the songs from his heart
He's a god, like Poseidon or Zeus

For years he got no recognition
Few people were paying admission
At venues he played
Little money he made
But persistency led to fruition

It was summer of '75
When Bruce and his band would arrive
With an album that still
Gives us many a thrill
When we see them performing it live

'Born to Run' hit the airwaves that year
And it soon was abundantly clear
That a star had arose
For the regular Joes
Less inclined to drink spritzers than beer

Many more beauty albums ensued
From this lunch bucket carrying dude
Who carved out quite a niche
And is now filthy rich
And who never gets heckled or booed

Bruce has been here for many great years
In a life full of blood, sweat and tears
With his songs we are blessed
So let's wish him the best
As old age and senility nears

Howard Stern

There's a radio guy known as Howard
With much freedom of speech he's empowered
On the air where he works
For the pay and the perks
He's a star, like the late Noel Coward

He's described as 'The King of all Media'
On the referencing site, Wikepedia
He's the sultan of shock
He gets paid just to talk
When he travels he books with Expedia

Howard knew as a pimple-faced youth
That he liked being rude and uncouth
So he flaunted convention
He savored dissension
And pulled many stunts as a goof

After high school to college he'd go
Where he got his own radio show
He reported the news
He was paying his dues
But the job didn't pay any dough

After earning his college degree
Howard knew where he wanted to be
Was the radio game
Seeking fortune and fame
Hoping people would laugh 'til they pee

Howard's now at the top of his trade
And a shitload of money he's made
With his candor and wit
Many nerves he has hit
By describing a spade as a spade

He's been criticized, censored and sued
For being outrageous and lewd
But his fans think he's great
Both the gay and the straight
Who've enjoyed all the venom he's spewed

Rod Stewart

Rod Stewart was born on a date
Nine months after his mother was late
With her monthly menstruation
Which led to gestation
And prompted her gut to inflate

Rod worked hard digging graves as a youth
Long before he got long in the tooth
Now he's semi-retired
Much wealth he's acquired
He never will spend all his loot

He played with Jeff Beck early on
In a stellar career that would spawn
Many songs on the charts
That are dear to the hearts
Of his groupies both hither and yon

Rod joined Faces and tasted success
With his singing and writing finesse
But a solo career
Is the path he would steer
That allowed him to truly impress

In the seventies Rod relocated
To the U.S. of A., where he mated
With many hot ladies
And drove a Mercedes
His manhood was often inflated

After that came unbridled prosperity
From his presence and vocal dexterity
Many records were sold
He was box office gold
For three decades, a show business rarity

Sly Stone

A funky musician named Sly
Was a brilliantly talented guy
On the show business scene
Not unlike Charlie Sheen
Much more often than not he was high

He was born in a north Texas town
Where he first was enticed by the sound
Of the rock and roll craze
In its earliest days
As it struggled to get off the ground

Before he was in to his teens
It was clear that he had in his genes
Many natural skills
That could pay many bills
He performed every night in his dreams

With some friends and two siblings he started
A band that would soon be regarded
As one of the best
As their journey progressed
On the course they haphazardly charted

As Sly and the Family Stone
They impressed both offshore and at home
With their numerous hits
And their penchant for glitz
They became very rich and well-known

With Everyday People they scored
A hit that propelled them toward
The success they had sought
They enjoyed it a lot
There was little they couldn't afford

But Sly was a troubled young dude
Who often adjusted his mood
With the help of cocaine
Which polluted his brain
His performances often were booed

In his prime, when he wasn't on dope
He epitomized freedom and hope
With the wonder and joy
Of a child with a toy
Who was often unable to cope

George Takei

A fellow we call George Takei
Has been out of the closet as gay
For a number of years
To his friends and his peers
Like Bill Shatner, who wears a toupee

George was five when the Second World War
Scared America deep to its core
When her judgement was blurred
The Takeis were interred
In a practice we now would deplore

At the end of the war George went back
To L.A. and developed a knack
For the thespian arts
And he landed some parts
Often playing an enemy Jap

He was stereotyped for a while
Like Jim Nabors, who played Gomer Pyle
Then the sixties arrived
And a show was contrived
Which would showcase his talent and style

Playing Sulu he took us through space
At a truly astonishing pace
Many courses he'd plot
With assistance from Scott
Who bought Romulan scotch by the case

On Star Trek George did very well
But his worth really started to swell
When 6 movies were spun
And released one by one
Each with fictional stories to tell

George Takei now has money galore
So he rarely makes films any more
Or have sex very often
His manhood has softened
He's yesterday's news, like Al Gore

Elizabeth Taylor

There once was a lady named Taylor
Who was featured in many a trailer
For movie releases
We loved her to pieces
Most men once aspired to nail 'er

She was born in the land of Great Britain
Where Shakespearean plays have been written
And a queen is revered
Which is silly and weird
And where drinking warm beer is befittin'

Liz was nine when she launched her career
And the path she was destined to steer
Earning fortune and fame
And artistic acclaim
With her power to charm and endear

In National Velvet she played
A damsel too young to get laid
Who prevails in a race
At a blistering pace
Velvet Brown is the gal she portrayed

MGM signed Miss Taylor post haste
And soon she was Hollywood based
Earning friends and esteem
While fulfilling her dream
Back when movies were made in good taste

Liz was married eight times in her life
On the Hollywood scene, which is rife
With impulsive romance
Where a bulge in the pants
Ends in serious marital strife

She made 62 films in her day
And was known from New York to Bombay
For her beauty and skill
And unselfish goodwill
She was worth every dime of her pay

Shirley Temple

A lady whose friends call her Shirley
Made dozens of films as a girly
She beguiled and endeared
Every time she appeared
With her mop of blond hair, which was curly

She was born long ago in L.A.
Not too far from Marina Del Rey
Where movies are made
And where starlets get laid
By producers who lead them astray

Shirley started to act as a tot
When her parents could see she was fraught
With much talent and flair
Not to mention great hair
So a lot of auditions were sought

When producers saw Shirley perform
To her agent they went in a swarm
Soon a contract was done
A career had begun
As a child took the movies by storm

In Little Miss Marker she starred
And was held in the highest regard
For the scenes she could make
In a singular take
Which for most is impossibly hard

In Heidi she charmed us to bits
As a gal using all of her wits
To escape from a captor
Who tricked and entrapped 'er
And gave her old Grandfather fits

Shirley Temple has now gone away
With her talent she blew us away
Stealing scene after scene
On the silvery screen
Where she earned every dime of her pay

Tiny Tim

A man that we called Tiny Tim
Was loaded with gusto and vim
He discovered a niche
With his ludicrous pitch
And his hair, which was needing a trim

He was born with the name Herbert Khaury
And aspired to musical glory
He played ukulele
He acted quite gaily
And soon was a national story

He scored big as a novelty act
As a guy who was patently whacked
Who had strangeness and zeal
And a cultish appeal
To make up for the talent he lacked

On Carson he married Miss Vicki
Who clearly was not very picky
But they soon were estranged
It was all pre-arranged
As a bit of nonsensical shticky

Tiny Tim was a true one-hit wonder
Whose 3 marriages all went asunder
He tip-toed through tulips
While sipping mint juleps
But soon he was losing his thunder

Tim would die in his 65th year
With the turn of the century near
He was wondrous and odd
And a bit of a clod
But we're glad for the time he was here

Tina Turner

A lady we call Tina Turner
Quite early in life was a yearner
To perform on the stage
For a livable wage
Or whatever her talent would earn 'er

In the 50's she lived in Missouri
But she wanted to split in a hurry
In a club she met Ike
Who stepped up to the mike
And would later be tried by a jury

Ike was gifted, but patently nuts
He treated his women like mutts
He and Tina got wed
But he filled her with dread
He inflicted contusions and cuts

Ike and Tina had numerous hits
They enjoyed all the money and glitz
But they fought all the time
For no reason or rhyme
So their marriage was soon on the fritz

So in '76 Tina fled
As her hubby was touched in the head
She went it alone
And got very well known
Making music and truckloads of bread

With her life and career both revived
Tina's time for success had arrived
People loved her to bits
All her records were hits
She would never again be deprived

Now it's many long years since the birth
Of a lady who's brimming with mirth
And persisted through pain
Very long may she reign
As the rock and roll queen of the Earth

Shania Twain

A talented gal known as Twain
Has seen days of both sunshine and rain
In the time she's been here
With her wonderful rear
And the music that comes from her brain

She was born in southwestern Ontario
In the British invasion scenario
And the decade of 'Nam
Which was based on a scam
Back when plastic was played on the stereo

As a child she had problems galore
Her mother and step-Dad were poor
And they often had fights
In the cold winter nights
Then awoke both hung over and sore

Shania began her career
And the course she was destined to steer
On her road to renown
In the bars in her town
Where the locals got hammered on beer

After high school she sang in a band
Known as 'Flirt' and they traveled the land
And she soon caught the eye
Of a disc jockey guy
Who decided to give her a hand

To Nashville they went to audition
Where sometimes a rookie musician
Can make a big splash
And significant cash
On the strength of a demo rendition

With her singular lyrics and sound
Soon Shania was studio bound
She sold records galore
Nice new outfits she wore
And a new Queen of Country was crowned

Mike Tyson

A heavyweight boxer named Mike
Has never been easy to like
He excelled with his fists
Which stick out from his wrists
But quite often his brain went on strike

In Brooklyn, New York he arrived
And a lot of bad times he survived
His old man was a lout
Who abruptly skipped out
Leaving Mike and his family deprived

He was mocked for the way that he spoke
And quite often his nose would get broke
Life was cruel and rough
So he had to be tough
Every day, from the time he awoke

As a teen he was frequently tested
And many a rival he bested
In fights on the street
Where he seldom got beat
And quite often his ass got arrested

But he learned how to channel his rage
For much more than the minimum wage
Cus D'Amato would train him
Reel in and restrain him
And foster his coming of age

Pretty soon he was beating contenders
And many unseasoned pretenders
He destroyed them with zeal
Both his hands were like steel
But he soon started going on benders

His missus alleged he abused her
And physically struck and contused her
With their marriage off course
She would file for divorce
When his antics no longer amused her

But by then Mike was heavyweight champ
With a penchant to act like a scamp
He got wasted a lot
All his girlfriends were hot
He got naked with many a tramp

When he lost to a bum known as Buster
He seemed to be lacking in bluster
He was sluggish and plump
In the waist and the rump
And he nearly got killed, like George Custer

Then his life went from weird to bizarre
When he took out a gal in his car
Things got bent out of shape
When she charged him with rape
Now she bears an emotional scar

After serving three years he was freed
When the terms of parole were agreed
He'd found God in the slammer
But still had bad grammar
And still liked to make people bleed

The promoters thought Tyson had changed
So a comeback was quickly arranged
He was still in demand
Though by some he was panned
And from three different spouses estranged

And then came that infamous fight
Where Mike Tyson decided to bite
The ear of Evander
Incurring his dander
In Vegas one mid-summer's night

The bite fight would screech to an end
A career that was hard to defend
Full of promise and waste
And of dubious taste
And more cash than most people can spend

Now Mike Tyson's retired and broke
And the punch line of many a joke
Once he reigned like a king
With the world on a string
Then he blew both his brain cells on coke

Sid Vicious

There once was a fellow named Sid
Who was troubled a lot as a kid
He arrived on this day
But he shortened his stay
With the stupid ass things that he did

Great Britain is where he was born
Where drinking warm beer is the norm
And where bowing to queens
Is ingrained in the genes
And the French are regarded with scorn

At birth he was John Simon Ritchie
Before he was vulgar and kitschy
And known for bad antics
And racy semantics
And getting a little bit tipsy

With The Flowers of Romance he started
The meandering course that he charted
To fame and success
And a fancy address
Before he was dearly departed

He performed with a few other bands
And helped them establish their brands
Though his playing was strong
He could not get along
So he didn't fit in to their plans

Johnny Rotten and Sid got together
And found they were birds of a feather
With The Pistols they played
Decent money they made
Decked out in torn blue jeans and leather

For a time Sid enjoyed notoriety
While flaunting the rules of society
But his partying ways
Caused a mental malaise
And an absence of sense and sobriety

Nancy Spungen came in to his life
And lived as his common-law wife
But she died in her bed
Quite profusely she bled
From repeated attacks with a knife

Sid Vicious was charged and made bail
But never was sentenced to jail
At the end of his rope
He OD'd on some dope
Then his lungs could no longer inhale

Jon Voight

A splendid old actor named Jon
Is known from New York to Ceylon
He was great in his day
Now he's wrinkled and gray
And his daughter looks hot in a thong

He arrived in New York long ago
Where it's easy to hire a 'ho
From the sex worker trade
If you're keen to get laid
By a gal who's a consummate pro

In high school Jon played his first part
Then in college he majored in art
And he earned a degree
In the land of the free
So he must have been reasonably smart

In the sixties he worked on TV
Filling network head honchos with glee
Later on he was seen
On the silvery screen
Where he earned a more sizable fee

Midnight Cowboy gave Jon his big chance
As a guy who was paid to romance
Many dried up old skanks
In the town of the Yanks
With the unit contained in his pants

In Deliverance Jon played a man
Who was part of a cover-up plan
When some yokels got dead
Who were both interbred
In a backwater hillbilly clan

All in all 60 movies he's made
Where a gamut of roles he's portrayed
As a hero or cad
Some were good, some were bad
But in each he's been handsomely paid

Christopher Walken

A fellow named Christopher Walken
Has a very unique way of talkin'
When he acts in a flick
Or in comedy schtick
When he's gone he won't soon be forgotten

He was born in the Empire State
Where the Rangers and Islanders skate
His Dad ran a store
Selling pastries galore
With a positive turnover rate

In the circus young Chris was employed
Where kids and their parents enjoyed
Many animal acts
While devouring snacks
Sold by vendors astutely deployed

After one year of college he quit
For the lure of the orchestra pit
And Broadway's bright lights
Where he soon earned his stripes
By the show business bug he was bit

To Hollywood Walken would go
Where his bank account started to grow
When his talent was seen
On the silvery screen
When he wasn't the star of the show

After proving his worth in his trade
In some trivial parts he portrayed
As a star he was cast
He was famous at last
And began to be handsomely paid

In Brainstorm he played Dr. Brace
Whose adrenalin started to race
During virtual sex
With his sensuous ex
As she sat on his virtual face

The Dead Zone was eerie and smart
Chris Walken was great in his part
As a guy who could see
What the future would be
And it wasn't a walk in the park

In Pulp Fiction he played a small role
Where he'd stashed a gold watch up his hole
In North Viet Nam
As her served Uncle Sam
When the commies were out of control

More than one hundred movies he's made
Making people amused and afraid
He has charmed and endeared
On the course that he's steered
And the solid foundation he's laid

Denzel Washington

An actor we know as Denzel
Is a star, just like Harvey Keitel
For his work he's been praised
In New York he was raised
In the era of Bobby Rydell

In college he earned a degree
A wordsmith he wanted to be
But he also had hopes
To be learning the ropes
As an actor in films or TV

Denzel studied theatre arts
After college and landed some parts
In commercials and plays
Drawing copious praise
For his talent and natural smarts

In St. Elsewhere he got his big break
And everything soon would be jake
Now Denzel was a star
With a shiny new car
And a lot of good money to make

After that, on the Hollywood scene
He displayed on the silvery screen
His remarkable skill
Giving millions a thrill
While lining his pockets with green

'Cry Freedom' was critically hailed
As a story where bias prevailed
In an African nation
With race segregation
Where Nelson Mandela was jailed

In 'The Pelican Brief' he portrayed
A guy in the newspaper trade
Who uncovered a plot
With a gal who was hot
And a boss who was hard to persuade

'Malcolm X' brought him kudos galore
As a man who was waging a war
And was loved and despised
'Til his tragic demise
But a difficult dude to ignore

In 'Training Day' Denzel became
A man with no scruples or shame
As a pilot in 'Flight'
He got high as a kite
Killed six people, then shouldered the blame

John Wayne

An American hero John Wayne
Fought for justice and talked very plain
In the movies he made
Then his life went to 'fade'
But his image is etched in our brain

He was born in a Midwestern State
Where they always have corn on their plate
His folks, Clyde and Molly
Were frugal yet jolly
And never stayed up very late

The Waynes up and moved to L.A.
Where the Angels and Rams used to play
His Dad filled prescriptions
For folks with afflictions
While Mom stayed at home for no pay

In high school his football ability
Including his strength and agility
Prompted scholarship offers
From colleges' coffers
So John had to pick a facility

USC was the school he attended
But his time there abruptly was ended
With his scholarship lost
He went out and got sauced
He was known for the elbows he bended

Fox Films gave young John his first parts
When he entered the theatre arts
Someone nicknamed him 'Duke'
He was cool as a cuke
And he soon stole a number of hearts

Nearly 200 movies he'd make
Many box office records he'd break
Plus the arms and the legs
Of some really bad eggs
In some wild western fights that were fake

Jack Webb

There once was a fellow named Webb
Who was known as a TV celeb
In his role as a cop
He was cream of the crop
In his 63rd year he dropped dead

He was born long ago in L.A.
The town where the Rams used to play
Where movies are made
And young hookers get paid
In exchange for a roll in the hay

Jack's old man was a bit of a prick
When his missus got pregnant he split
And he never returned
To the family he spurned
When he went on a permanent trip

After high school Jack landed a post
On a radio show on the coast
A detective he played
Like Gene Hunt and Sam Spade
In his work he was fully engrossed

Later Dragnet was heard on the air
Where Joe Friday was Jack's nom de guerre
For eight years it was on
Many listeners were drawn
To a cop who was savvy but square

The show then appeared on TV
Where people were able to see
How police work is done
In the yarns that were spun
Filling millions of people with glee

So I offer a tribute to Jack
Who possessed a particular knack
For portraying a guy
Who was deadpan and dry
And gave bad guys a kick in the sac

Vanna White

A middle aged lady named Vanna
On TV plays a second banana
With no talent or skill
Now she's over the hill
But alive, unlike Lady Diana

She was born with no hair on her pate
In a former Confederate State
Where the winters are mild
And tobacco grows wild
And they often have grits on their plate

Vanna's father was not very nice
He abandoned his wife in a trice
After Vanna arrived
But she wasn't deprived
Of good food or parental advice

In Playboy young Vanna was seen
When she still was an innocent teen
She gave acting a shot
But she wasn't so hot
On TV or the silvery screen

But she later discovered her niche
And she's gotten quite famous and rich
As a glorified shill
Oozing glee and goodwill
On a game show with products to pitch

Bruce Willis

A man who is known as Bruce Willis
Makes movies designed to fulfill us
With action galore
They are rarely a bore
Most enrapture, bedazzle and thrill us

New Jersey is where he was reared
Where Chris Christie is now being smeared
He closed down some lanes
For political gains
In a stunt that was nasty and weird

Bruce stuttered a lot as a youth
His schoolmates were mean and uncouth
With their venomous cracks
And malicious attacks
Now they're dead, or quite long in the tooth

But he spoke very well when he played
Parts in plays, where he wasn't afraid
To deliver his lines
At their prearranged times
Much composure and calm he displayed

After high school he went to auditions
For various Broadway renditions
And he landed some roles
In pursuit of his goals
He was loaded with lofty ambitions

Bruce moved west to L.A. for the chance
To allow his career to advance
In the realm of TV
Where there's no guarantee
One will ever be given a glance

He found work right away on the coast
In his trade he was fully engrossed
His Moonlighting part
Was well written and smart
Of the town he was clearly the toast

After that there were offers galore
Quite a future the man had in store
In Die Hard he shone
As a fellow named John
In a movie that millions adore

Death Becomes Her he did later on
Playing Ernest, who humped Goldie Hawn
Causing marital strife
Meryl Streep played his wife
But the film was a bit of a yawn

His best movie of all was Pulp Fiction
A splendidly raunchy depiction
Of life on the edge
With a jump from a ledge
By a boxer who'd caused a conniption

Oprah Winfrey

Oprah Winfrey's been known to inflate
With her penchant for putting on weight
But discovered her niche
Now she's famous and rich
Living large on her lavish estate

She grew up in the town of Milwaukee
Where the weather's conducive to hockey
As a child she was sad
Lots of trauma she had
So her road to abundance was rocky

To Nashville she moved to escape
From the pain and the peril of rape
At the hands of some kin
Who were guilty as sin
She was not in a good mental state

When she went to reside with her Dad
A much easier time Oprah had
As a student she shone
To the stage she was drawn
And developed a gift for the gab

While in college she worked on the air
Reading news and exhibiting flair
And no shortage of smarts
In the radio arts
And ate many a chocolate eclair

And then she discovered her mission
In life when she made the transition
To the talk show domain
Which was foreign terrain
She contended with stiff competition

What ensued was unbridled success
Lots of cash and a fancy address
As her audience grew
She's a publisher too
Sincer her magazine first went to press

Natalie Wood

A lady named Natalie Wood
At her job was exceedingly good
Once she worked with James Dean
On the silvery screen
When he played a new boy in the 'hood

She was born in the city of Frisco
Before the invention of disco
Where the 'Niners play ball
In the Summer and Fall
Up north from San Luis Obispo

She began playing roles as a child
When the language in movies was mild
When no nude scenes were shot
To enliven the plot
And no buxom young stars got defiled

As Natalie grew and matured
More and more she beguiled and allured
In the parts that she played
Hefty profits were made
And voluminous chubbies were spurred

Robert Wagner she wed, but she'd dump him
When others had started to hump him
They later remarried
His baby she carried
When flaccid she knew how to plump him

But Bob was a bit of a louse
And quite often a booze swilling souse
Who spent time on his yacht
Where he partied a lot
Which did not sit so well with his spouse

One night Natalie fell in the sea
And drowned while attempting to flee
The wrath of her mate
Who was very irate
On their boat she did not want to be

The story her husband related
For which he's been widely berated
Was believed by the fuzz
And still causes a buzz
When the facts of the case are debated

Many still think her husband's a rotter
For leaving his wife in the water
To punish her ass
When she gave him some sass
Then insisting he desperately sought her

Tammy Wynette

A lady named Tammy Wynette
Sang songs about pain and regret
'Til the day that she died
With her man by her side
All her husbands could form a quintet

She was born in northwest Mississippi
Where moonshine is drank when it's nippy
And where peanuts are grown
From the seeds that are sown
By the makers of Planters and Skippy

Tammy wasn't aware of her Dad
He passed on from a tumor he had
Then 8-month old Tammy
Moved in with her Granny
Until she could get her own pad

She sang gospel a lot as a teen
On her road to becoming the queen
Of the country domain
Earning fortune and fame
Which was always her ultimate dream

Tammy started by paying her dues
In clubs serving coffee and booze
Then to Memphis she went
And began her ascent
To a chorus of glowing reviews

By the seventies Tammy was known
As a gal with a singular tone
With Stand By Your Man
Superstardom began
And she purchased an opulent home

She hooked up with George Jones for a while
Their duets made their managers smile
As the dollars rolled in
They were living in sin
Then they walked down the conjugal aisle

Tammy died in her 56th year
But in the short time she was here
She won millions of hearts
With her songs on the charts
As we happily cried in our beer

Warren Zevon

Warren Zevon was one of a kind
With a dark and exceptional mind
He was stylish and bold
Many stories he told
Until sadly he ran out of time

He exuded a curious joy
Like a child who was given a toy
Then would smash it apart
With ill will in his heart
He was just an Excitable Boy

At 16 he quit school and moved west
To L.A. and embarked on a quest
To regale with his tunes
In the clubs and saloons
And to hopefully feather his nest

He succeeded in reaching his goal
Of filling a musical role
When his skills came to light
From the way he could write
With the genius ingrained in his soul

With his songs about anguish and war
He sold records at home and offshore
With his singular style
And his mischievous smile
He had money and groupies galore

With Werewolves of London he scored
On the charts, and his revenue soared
His commercial success
Bought a fancy address
That he never before could afford

He wrote of a man with no head
Who still walked even though he was dead
In search of the man
Who had shot him and ran
When he found him he filled him with lead

Warren battled with demons and won
And expired when still fairly young
At his home in L.A.
On a very sad day
At the end of a wonderful run

Lightning Source UK Ltd.
Milton Keynes UK
UKOW04f0627071214

242741UK00005B/452/P